POPULAR FLOWERING PLANTS

POPULAR FLOWERING PLANTS

H. L. V. FLETCHER

DRAKE PUBLISHERS INC

NEW YORK

Published in 1972 *by*
DRAKE PUBLISHERS INC
381 Park Avenue South, New York, N.Y. 10016

U.S. copyright registered 1972
©H. L. V. Fletcher 1971

Printed in the United States of America

CONTENTS

ILLUSTRATIONS

(following page 32)

ILLUSTRATIONS

Chapter 1: THE ROSE

There are a few gardens here and there in which no Roses at all are grown. A few but not many.

Anne of Austria, wife of Louis XIII of France had such an antipathy to them that she could not bear even a picture of one. The Duke of Guisé turned round and walked in the opposite direction even at the sight of a Rose. But apart from those two I have never heard of a gardener who said he (or she) did not like Roses. It is the most popular and the most loved flower in the world. It is on a pinnacle, it stands alone, it is a synonym for beauty, for form, grace, perfume, elegance: it has all the virtues and no vices save that it has prickles—no Rose without a thorn (only there is)—a fact noted by many, but (in English literature, anyhow) first written down by Shakespeare, then Milton, and even they were only pointing a moral. It has been a favourite, both in the garden and in the wild as far back as we have records, and there were as beautiful blooms growing in the gardens of 2,000 B.C. (and earlier) as there are likely to be in A.D. 2,000.

There are species native to practically every country in the northern hemisphere and one wonders why Nature never spared one or two to grow south of the equator. But—so far as I have ever been able to discover—she did not and what the reason can be is a mystery, but perhaps no more a mystery than why there are no marsupials north of it. Of course man has corrected the omission long since.

I don't know how many species, or wild types, there are and I have a feeling that nobody else does either because the figures the botanists offer vary from about 100 to about 200 and that is a wide gap. Anyhow it does not matter (except to botanists). The fact that does matter is that over thousands of years the wild Roses have been interbreeding freely giving rise to new types and the end (as far as we are concerned) is the glorious coloured, scented, shapely blooms that grace our gardens today. I would be ashamed to quote again Walter de la Mare's passing thought about the centuries it has taken for the Rose to develop but it is a good thought and good poetry and you are pretty sure to know it.

It doesn't really matter. In the Rose garden—in a few—grow a handful of species, or near species, from which the near-perfect modern hybrid tea has descended: *Rosa damascena, Rosa gallica,* the China Rose, our own Dog Rose and Sweet Briar. Bourbons and Teas and Noisettes, and all the rest, and if you read up the experts they will trace out the family tree for you. But the ancestry is complicated and often the experts do not agree with each other and I have given up wondering at it, and puzzling my head over it. I've got my Roses and from what strange intermarriages they came doesn't worry me any more. After all, some of us must have come of some queer mesalliances in one period or another, but we are what we are. So are the Roses what *they* are. And very nice, too.

I bought my first two Rose bushes a long time ago, so long that I am a bit touchy about quoting figures, but I paid 6d. each for them so that gives the show away! I lost 50 per cent of my stock. That was a yellow, popular at the time, called Florence L. Izzard, but the other 50 per cent was a very beautiful bicolour, Queen Alexandra and she is with me still. Not very vigorous, mind; and I too am not what I was; but she gives me a few blooms every season. It is pleasant to have plenty of Rose bushes in the garden, but the advantage of having only one is that you appreciate every petal to the full. The next year I had six more trees—still in the poor-relation, sixpenny class and I really did feel I was becoming something of a Rose-grower then.

Two of those bushes I still have, hybrid perpetuals, Hugh Dickson and Frau Karl Druschki. More of those later perhaps. They flourish like the green bay tree, and look not a day older than when they came out of their wrappings, which alas is more than can be said for most of us!

The height of perfection has been reached in the modern hybrid tea. It may be that better Roses will be developed, but it is difficult to imagine them. New varieties come along constantly and to make room for them some of the old inhabitants drop out. That in a way is the chief fault of the modern kinds: impermanence. Each year the breeders put a few new varieties on the market. I don't know how many of these good men there are around, but counting the Continental raisers and American ones there must be a regiment of them. If each produces two new beauties a year (some introduce more) the market gets sort of choked and the ones you bought three years ago vanish and the place thereof shall know them no more. It would not matter only some of the novelties are not really better than the old inhabitants. Only newer. That's progress. I suppose it does not matter. I await the season when the sellers throw away *all* their stock to make way for the flood of novelties. And that year the breeders will have decided to give it a miss for one season. No Roses for sale. Ah well, it will be a change! And that's as good as a rest.

Of course there are other types besides the hybrid teas. Their immediate predecessors were the hybrid perpetuals. The hybrid tea was said to be bred from the hybrid perpetuals crossed with a Tea, which got their name because they were thought to have a scent of tea. That may be so though I have a feeling the union that led to the progeny was not as simple as that.

Hybrid perpetuals were the Roses of our Victorian ancestors. They did not flower perpetually, but they did, unlike some garden Roses of the time, flower more than once, and with luck Grandpapa had some nice blooms in autumn. I would not claim that perpetuals are popular any more but most growers keep a small stock of the best. They would not do that if they were not worth growing. They *are* worth growing.

I have four: Hugh Dickson, Frau Karl Druschki, Mrs John Laing and (I think) Georg Arends. Frau Karl Druschki is an outstanding Rose. It is, I am sure, the finest white bloom in commerce. It lacks scent but in shape and form, strength and size it is perfect. Mrs John Laing is a lovely rose colour and has such a wonderful perfume it makes up for the Frau not having any. The

best of us have our faults and Mrs Laing's is that she can't abide
wet and cold, and in such weather will often not open her buds.
Hugh Dickson's is that the bud is so heavy that the perfectly-
formed velvety-crimson flowers tend to bend the stems when
they get full of rain.

I don't know what fault Georg Arends has unless it is that as
the flowers mature the colour (which is a bright shade of rose)
fades to a not very pleasing pink.

Perpetuals are usually very resistant to disease and they are
particularly strong growers, often sending up new shoots six feet
or more high. They will enjoy good feeding and should have it.
The way to grow them is to prune out as much as possible of the
older wood at the end of the season—or in spring in cold districts.
Every new long shoot then is arched over and the tip pegged to
the ground. Every bud on each arched stem will produce a
young shoot and every shoot a bloom or group of blooms. The
result is quite an eye-opener to those who have never seen this
method before. A pegged hybrid perpetual can produce, literally, hundreds and hundreds of blooms, and on a warm sunny
day when they are free with their fragrance each bush is an indescribable mixture of colour and scent.

Discerning growers who would like something new (old really!) to try could do worse than grow a bed of the perpetuals.
As for varieties it all depends on what the nurseryman has to offer. My four are as good as you will ever find, but six more good
ones are Baroness Rothschild, pink; Blue Boy (a modern one
this which is rather unusual, introduced in 1958), reddish violet;
Ferdinand Pickard, striped, crimson on white; Prince Camille
de Rohan, dark crimson; Reine des Violettes, lilac purple; Ulrich
Brunner, red.

The perpetuals, as Rose history goes, are modern. Behind them
stands a host of very mixed types—the long and the short and the
tall as it were. A few nurseries grow these older ones and a few
people have collected them and written books about them. There
is no single label under which they can be grouped though I think
the title Shrub Rose is now becoming generally accepted. That
title can be taken as synonymous with Old Fashioned Roses and
Bush Roses, but it is as shrubs they should be grown, for only a

few are much use for the modern Rose bed, while as shrubs they are first rate.

Their chief drawback is that the majority bloom once only in the year. Most other shrubs do, if it comes to that. Generally there is a crop sometime in June and July that lasts a few weeks, then a tailing-off for a week or two ('the last rose of summer' period), and then you must be content with foliage and, in some cases, a crop of hips.

I don't think they have any other bad points. Very few have the perfect shape of the modern hybrid teas, a few are unashamedly blousy, but most are very much more strongly scented than any modern ones. They are usually vigorous and will do well in quite poor soil so they are often suitable for gardens where modern Roses do not do well. Also they are resistant to disease, and flourish without any attention whatever. (In fairness I'll add that most hybrid teas would too if their owners would only leave them alone!)

For convenience the Shrub Roses have been divided into groups. These groups are often made to sound as if they are species or wild types, the originals, as it were, but they are not. Some of them are complete mixtures and they would not blush if they admitted they hadn't any idea who their parents were. I am an unscientific non-botanist so I accept the groupings as I find them in the best catalogues and in books on the subject.

I know of twelve main groups. *Rosa alba* is an old Rose that has been grown in England since the Middle Ages. They grow into big bushes, their flowers are usually pale shades, they are strongly scented and flower in June and July.

Bourbon Roses are a cross between China and Damask Roses. That we do know for they came from an accidental cross on the island of Reunion and only those two grew there. The best Bourbons flower at all times, in favourable circumstances, from May to December, and they have a marvellous fragrance. They have a good share in the parentage of the hybrid perpetuals and undoubtedly are responsible for the perpetualness and fragrance of that group.

Rosa centifolia, the Cabbage Rose. It has always been believed that this was one of the oldest in existence, the Rose of a Hundred

Petals, the Rose of Roman feasts, described by Herodotus, by Theophrastus, by Pliny. Gerard grew it in his Holborn garden in the sixteenth century, Parkinson wrote of it in his *Paradisus*, the herbalist Nicholas Culpeper told us what ills it would alleviate or cure . . . I could continue in this vein but alas and alack—along comes the scientist and proves, without shadow of a doubt, that the Cabbage Rose can at the most be only a couple of hundred years old. So where are we?

Let's forget origins. Plant a bush whatever its ancestry. It flowers as freely, it smells as sweet whether it is two years old or two thousand.

The Moss Rose. This is a sport from the Cabbage Rose, having a growth of fine hairs, often sticky, all over the buds and stems. This 'moss' gives the plant its character, otherwise it is similar in colour, scent and vigour to its parent.

Rosa damascena is the Damask Rose, and (if the botanists will permit me) the Damascena is Damascus from where the Crusaders brought the plant to Europe. This strongly scented flower is the Rose of Attar of Roses, the Rose of the Persian poets. There is, or was, a bush growing on Omar Khayyam's grave in Naishapur. Seeds from it were brought to Kew about 1884 and from one of the seedlings a cutting was planted on Edward FitzGerald's grave, and cuttings from that one have been named Omar Khayyam, and descendants of those are on sale at a few nurseries.

One of the Damasks, Rose des Quatre Saisons, flowers in autumn as well as in summer.

Rosa gallica. I take it by the name that these are the Roses of Gaul. In fact they are sometimes called the French Rose. But they are far older than any French civilisation for it is believed they were grown earlier than 1,000 B.C. in Persia, where they were used in medicines. In Europe they were cultivated in medieval gardens, again for medical purposes, and then the town of Provins, near Paris, cornered the industry, and for a long period Provins was the centre of this trade. Hence another name, Provins Rose (*not* Provence Rose though, that is another story). Dutch and French growers raised hundreds of varieties and in the early nineteenth century they were as popular and as widely grown as hybrid teas are today. Some growers say they were better in colour, in shape and in scent. They flower only in June and July though.

The Austrian Briars. These are not as striking as many groups. Their significance is that they were used in the breeding of Pernetiana Roses, named after a M. Pernet, a French raiser. We no longer hear much about Pernetiana Roses as such, but, if I remember rightly they were used to develop the hybrid teas in many respects especially in the strong dark green foliage and some new rich shades.

The Musk Rose, *Rosa moschata*. This is an old favourite; a flower of Tudor gardens and well known to Shakespeare. The scent was famous in his day and is still rich in ours. Many good modern Shrub Roses have been bred by cross-pollination with this group.

Noisette Roses are supposed to be hybrids between Musk and China Roses, though it is doubtful if it is as simple as that. The only time it matters is when individual growers put them in different classes and you fail to find them in his catalogue. For instance one merchant puts the delightful Gloire de Dijon down as a Noisette, whereas it is probably a (nearly!) pure Tea Rose. One of the loveliest climbers and least grown—Maréchal Neil is a Noisette, and another is the vigorous William Allen Richardson.

The Sweet Briars are botanically *Rosa rubiginosa*. The flowers are poor as a rule but the fragrance of the leaves is one of the best in English gardens. Sweet Briars make a good hedge or screen.

Rosa rugosa. Rose growers know this best as a stock on which to bud other Roses, but it suckers a lot and is not a really good stock. It is a native of China mainly. It is a good shrub, making a tall spreading bush with very thorny stems, light green leaves and big single flowers with wide papery petals. These are followed by large roundish hips. Some of the hybrids of the Rugosas are very beautiful shrubs.

Rosa spinosissima is the very thorny Scots Briar often found wild on dunes and barren places. The original type had creamy single flowers but there are lovely hybrids available now with double blooms in various colours.

There is another group of Roses usually listed in the catalogues as Modern Shrub Roses or some such title. These are mainly hybrids and so much cross-breeding has been done to get them that it is doubtful if their true parentage is known. Never mind; human beings like to know from whom they are descended but Roses don't care! The only drawback is from the buyer's point of view, who, poor fellow, out of all the multitude available scarcely knows what to ask for or what to plant. Especially when he only has room for a dozen—or less.

If this were a book about Roses only I would give plenty of lists—not complete ones; I doubt if there are any—but lots of choice of all the best. As it is the gardener must study the catalogues and visit the nurseries. But I know many who do appreciate pin-pointed guidance and for their sake I will offer the names of a dozen Shrub Roses one of each group that I would plant myself if I were starting a collection.

ROSA ALBA   Felicity Parmentier. Cream and pink.

BOURBON ROSE   Zephyrine Drouhin. Carmine.

ROSA CENTIFOLIA   Old Cabbage Rose. (In spite of what I have written earlier the date of introduction is given as 1583!)

MOSS ROSE   Blanche Moreau. White, occasionally striped.

DAMASK ROSE   York and Lancaster. Striped pink and white. If you do not like striped Roses plant Quatre Saisons.

ROSA GALLICA   *R. gallica officinalis,* the Apothecaries Rose. Crimson.

AUSTRIAN BRIAR   Persian Yellow.

MUSK ROSE   Felecca. Pink.

NOISETTES   Maréchal Neil (to be grown under glass).

SWEET BRIAR   Lady Penzance. Orange. Single.

RUGOSAS   *R. rugosa rubra.* Red.

ROSA SPINOSISSIMA   Double yellow Scots Briar. A three foot shrub.

All nurserymen who go in for old-fashioned Roses in a big way grow and sell many of the species. These are the wild Roses of other lands and should be the originals from which the various hybrids have sprung. But they never are. Hybridising—cross-breeding that is—has gone on as freely in the wild as in the nurseries. Still, these are the plants collected in the wild (though the hybridists soon get to work on them!) and many are the work of Nature rather than of Rose growers. Out of the vast number available a few dozen have been chosen for gardens.

Except for the dedicated enthusiast I do not think all of them are worth a place in the garden. I would not, for instance, plant our own Dog Rose, *Rosa canina*. It is a pretty little thing in hedgerows and woods and sometimes you see a flower of good rich colour. But the blossoms are too fleeting and the growth too wild. It can be grown into a first-class hedge, though. In one of my own hedges a seedling has sprung up. It has purple stems and creamy white flowers with gold stamens and for a few weeks in summer is a very pretty sight. The stems ramble more wildly than any rambler but are easily trimmed back and the laurels do not complain. I have, in the same hedge, a couple of Sweet Briars which are hardly noticeable except on a warm damp day when I have known them to stop passers-by in their tracks and they cry like Walter de la Mare:

> 'It is wild roses
> Do smell so winsomely,
> And winy briar too' says I
> 'That in these thickets be.'

My favourite wild Rose is the Chinese R. *moyesii* which has dark red flowers, leaves with many small leaflets and long bottle-shaped hips.

R. *hugonis*, with yellow flowers and dark hips is another worth growing, so is the yellow R. *cantabrigiensis* (though that really is a hybrid). R. *sancta* is said to have come from Abyssinian temples. It has crinkled pink petals, quite large, which fade to white; R. *paulii* grows into an enormous bush which is covered with white flowers.

All those are worth having but with the species it is like taking a wife (or husband). Better have a good look before you choose.

No great originality is shown in the way most of us grow our bushes. We don't get past Roses-in-the-Rosebed. They always grew that way: they always will. So we buy a dozen—or a hundred—bushes and into the formal oblong-cut-out-of-grass they go. Up to a hundred we probably talk of the Rose bed—or beds; where there are thousands we'll call it the Rose garden.

Years ago I used to make a trellis of straight larch uprights and the crooked pieces of oak that I could cut from a branch off one of the many fine trees that grew near the house. The trellis was a strong firm structure—it had to be—and I enjoyed making it and got a sort of craftsman's satisfaction out of looking at it. Ramblers were planted by the posts and tied in to the framework and they were pleasant all the year and they flowered in glory for a couple of months in summer. I made similar supports for climbing teas, and grew more on arches. Our house was rather severely flat so I made a rustic arch to stand over the front door and a Tausendschön (a thornless rambler—I haven't seen one for years) grew up one side and a vigorous Cabbage Rose the other. Roses round the door, indeed! And very nice, too!

At the back of my main bed I put seven foot larch poles and grew ramblers and climbers on them. I grew teas in 8½ inch and 9½ inch pots in my little greenhouse and so had blooms in early spring. I grew a rambler in a pot, and kept it down to about five feet. Mind I had the Rose-growing fever pretty badly at that time!

You can have them anywhere and everywhere. Some floribundas in tubs for the steps or the porch. A pergola over a paved or gravel walk is a formidable thing to construct but what a lovely sight when completed and furnished. I have known the most vigorous kinds grown on old or dead trees. One man I heard of (I did not see this) grew ramblers and clematis mixed on a bank and left both to trail at their own sweet wills.

So grow your Roses in the formal bed, but when that is as perfect as it can be, look round for fresh worlds to conquer.

As far as culture is concerned luckily the Rose is not fussy. It will grow anywhere and in any soil. It will grow better, much better, in some places than in others, but there are few places where it will not grow at all, and I think we can take it that the more trouble we take the better the results will be.

The position is important. It should be open and get plenty of light and plenty of sun and warmth. I do not think a south aspect is necessarily the best. Roses will do quite well facing east; probably better facing south or west. But they should be out of the prevailing wind. Two things are murder to almost any plants:

one is a draught, the sort of thing you get when a current of air is funnelled up to and across the plants. You often get this between a garden wall (or fence) and a house wall. The other is a strong wind that lashes the trees from side to side, tearing at the buds and blooms as if it would snatch them off, ripping petals against thorns. If the position where you want to plant the bushes is draughty or windy look round for another; if there isn't another put in screens and shelter belts without delay. If you will use growing things for screens use some woven-wood or over-lap sections until they are established.

Soil matters but it does not matter as much as some experts have tried to make us believe. Very few soils are perfect and the imperfect can always be improved. If it is *very* heavy—and Roses will *not* grow in clay unless it is made suitable, then it must be limed and winter-dug and have a lot of manure and compost dug in—those two first—then anything that will lighten it and warm it and bring it into nice workable condition: leaves, leaf-mould, peat, hop manure and grit; road sweepings from an untarred road are excellent.

If the soil is light then, curiously, you add almost the same materials, manure, compost, leaves, leaf-mould, and peat. They will put humus in it, darken it, give it body and that clean sponginess that is the hall-mark of healthy soil. Straw helps in soils of this nature and the lawn mowings of a few summers will work wonders.

A Rose garden, once planned and planted, will last a lifetime without needing any major work done to it if the soil has been well prepared, but a little care is called for at certain seasons to keep everything going smoothly.

I have worked out my own programme to a minimum, giving me time to look at my flowers rather than labour over them. It starts in autumn. Any time early in autumn I fork the ground over. Don't be too rough on the roots but do not worry when they do get broken. Call it root-pruning and pretend you meant to break them! Dig with a border fork and turn the soil over in lumps. Leave the surface as rough as possible, partly for aeration but mainly so that the winter frosts can work on it.

In November I give each bush a generous handful of bonemeal.

If I can get it I give a top-dressing of manure but compost is almost as good; some say it is better.

Many gardeners prefer to spread the manure in spring. This is probably best on light soils but mine is heavy. Manure on the beds in spring can hinder spring cultivation of the soil. Also my enthusiasm started after reading Dean Hole's classic, *The Book of the Rose,* and the Dean's advice was to top-dress with manure in autumn, so it became a habit and I have grown too obstinate to change!

There is little to do now until spring except look over the bushes after gales and heel back into place any that have rocked holes round their necks so that they are rolling about like walking sticks in an umbrella stand.

In March or April the bushes are pruned. Sometimes I prune lightly but in my cold district early shoots are usually spoiled by late frosts so it pays to prune hard, cutting all stems down to three or four buds from the ground. Now you see the benefit of the autumn forking over; the soil when dry breaks down at the touch of a hoe to a lovely light, loose tilth, and the frost-broken manure mixes in easily.

The bushes, with the bonemeal and manure, will not lack plant foods, but they may need a little extra nourishment for late summer and autumn blooms, and as it must be given well ahead of when it is needed it should be given in spring. A light dressing of any good general fertiliser will do, but many firms have their own formulae and as a rule these are just that little bit better. I like a little blood manure: it is quickly absorbed; if it is spread on the beds and hoed in it results in healthy stems, strong rich leaves and well-coloured blooms.

By June the flower buds are swelling at the tip of every stem. I used to let them all develop into flowers: I could not bear to part with a single one! Nowadays, except on floribunda and polyantha types I generally disbud, leaving the bud at the tip of the stem and removing the ones beneath it. In this way I get a much finer bloom and really they come along so swiftly in high summer that the discarded buds are hardly missed.

And actually that is all the work I do. I suppose there should be a few words on when I spray and what for and with what. But I do not spray—ever or with anything. I have not used a poisonous spray in my garden for more than thirty years. And the garden is not riddled with pests nor ruined by disease. Caterpillars like the little leaf-rolling one I pick off, while the birds eat all the aphids.

If I find a bush with Black Spot I give the soil a good dressing of sulphate of potash to make good any potash deficiency then burn such leaves as I can gather. A heavy mulch of lawn mowings helps to keep the spores in banishment.

If sprays must be used I recommend vegetable and non-poisonous ones, derris or pyrethrum for greenfly, Bordeaux mixture for Black Spot and flowers of sulphur for mildew. Poisons often kill off the bees and other beneficial creatures as well as foes. I'm wary of anything that has CAUTION printed in the directions for use.

That great non-traveller, Sir John Mandeville said that Roses first came into existence at Bethlehem. They were going to burn to death an innocent girl, but she prayed and the fire went out . . . 'those branches that were brenninge became red Roses and those branches that were not kindled became white Rosiers full of white roses, and those were the fyrst Rosiers that any man sawe.'

A more ancient legend tells that the flower arose from the blood of Adonis when he was killed by the wild boar; yet another that there were white Roses only but they were stained red by the feet of Venus as they were torn by thorns as she tried to rescue him.

And so on. Rhodanthe, Queen of Corinth, was turned into a tree that bore the flower.

There are other tales. Mohammedans associate the flower with the Prophet . . . There is no lack of legends. In fact there are so many that it is difficult to remember them all.

Pleasant conceits . . . yet we should not smile too much. Some of them have been taken very seriously in their time, and one thing led to another. The white Rose was the emblem of the Jacobites and they used it as a secret name for the king 'over the water'.

'Here's to him that's awa', Willie,
Here's to him that's awa', Willie,
And here's to the flow'r that I lo'e best.
The Rose that's like the sna'.'

And why should the Jacobites adopt the White Rose? Well,
Cupid bribed Harpocrates, god of Silence, not to betray the love
affairs of Venus. So it became the badge of silence, the closed bud
was the emblem of the sealed mouth. They carved Roses in inns
and in banqueting halls as a reminder not to repeat what was
heard when men talked too much in their cups. You find it everywhere. There is a Dutch couplet that translates:

'All that is done here, under the Rose
Leave it here and do not divulge it.'

And so to the gentlemen, booted and spurred, plotting to bring
the Stuarts back to the throne.

There was once a movement (I suppose it was not as definite as
that) to give the flower a religious association. And some of our
earliest poems make it the flower of the Virgin Mary.

'The flour sprong in heye Bedlem,
That is bothe bright and schen:
The rose is Mary, hevene qwen,
Out of her bosum the blosme sprong.'

But it had already become the flower of earthly pleasure, the
flower of wine and feasts, and the honour passed to the Lily.

The herbalists valued the flower as much as anyone. Even as
far back as Pliny . . . 'Rose juice is used for the ears, sores in the
mouth, the gums, as a gargle for the tonsils, for the stomach,
uterus, rectal trouble, headache . . .'

A fair list but it is only a tithe of them . . . Stomach ache, the
spitting of blood, erysipelas, sore eyes, 'complaints of the belly or
intestines', hypochondria, the biting of a mad dog . . . a full list
would run to many pages. We smile but Rose hip syrup is one
of the richest sources of Vitamin C, while in the *Daily Mail* for
March 22, 1962 there is an account of how '. . . at the King Edward VII Memorial Chest Hospital, Hertford Hill, Warwick, no

heart operation begins until the Rose ritual (placing a Yellow Rose on the heart-lung machine) has been completed.'

The Rose cost 1s. 9d. but the effect on the morale of the patient was incalculable.

Not only Roses for medicine, Roses for food also. Gerard gives a recipe for Conserve of Roses—which I take to be a sort of jam. Sir Hugh Platt tells how they can be preserved whole like a sot of candied fruit. Princess Elizabeth, daughter of Charles I has left us her recipe for Rose-flavoured cake. In Bunyard's *Old English Roses* there is a recipe for Rose Jelly, while at various times I have seen recipes for Rose Jam, Rose Petal filling for sandwiches, Rose water, and Candied Rose petals.

There seems to be no end to the list of uses for this paragon of flowers. As far as I know, no member of the Rose family is poisonous (how different it would be if I were writing of the Buttercups—*ranunculaceae,* or the potato-tobacco tribe—*solanaceae!*) so we ought to try some of these recipes. Though I suppose the next thing would be tinned Roses, which is a horrible thought!

Of course the pleasantest use is the making of the perfume Attar of Roses. It seems to have been discovered at a wedding of one of the Mogul Emperors, Jehan Ghir. Canals in the gardens had been covered with Rose petals and as he and his bride, the beautiful Nur-jehan walked on the banks they noticed an oily substance floating on the water. This oil was collected, pure Attar, and the perfume was named Attar-jehanhiri, the Perfume of Jehan Ghir.

Now the manufacture of this exquisite scent has become a matter of commerce. Growing Roses for it has gone on in various countries, generally in warm or hot ones since the sun seems to coax out the perfume at its strongest. A century ago it was carried on—may still be—in Bengal. In Europe Bulgaria went in for Rose growing for the making of the Attar and in France the district around Grasse seems to have become the chief centre.

It is expensive stuff. Thirty Roses, so I have been told, produce only one drop of the precious essence.

Chapter 2: LILIES

There is little doubt that the Madonna Lily, *Lilium candidum,* is the oldest Lily in cultivation. There is evidence from its use in decorations of various sorts, on vases, in frescoes and so on that it was grown thousands of years B.C. There is even evidence that it is a survivor from before the Ice Age so it may be one of the oldest flowers in existence.

It probably owes its spread over Europe to the Romans. It was certainly cultivated by them, for the poet Virgil mentions it: probably others did too. No doubt they valued it for its beauty but all Lilies, from the earliest times had many medicinal uses, and there is a story that the juice would cure corns, and the legions took it on their journeyings not so that they could plant it and enjoy its flowers but to use it in doctoring their poor calloused feet.

Apparently it was the Venerable Bede who first made this flower the emblem of the purity of the Virgin Mary, but there appears to have been some earlier records associating them for there is a second century tradition that her tomb was visited three days after her death and it was empty except for some Roses and Lilies. In art most notable pictures which show the Virgin show also Lilies and this symbolising went on all down the centuries, at least until the pre-Raphaelites. I don't think the name Madonna Lily was used until the last century. In fact not all the Lilies in sacred pictures may have been Madonnas. There were other white species and to an artist a white Lily would be a white Lily. But, undoubtedly *L. candidum* was the first.

By the sixteenth century men were appreciating Lilies as flowers, and growing them in gardens for their beauty. But earlier, in the troubled Middle Ages, especially through the Wars of the

Roses, decorative gardening was not part of the English way of
life and most plants grown were for food or medicine. And of
course when settled peaceful times came to mean pleasant
gardens the herbal uses lingered, even persisted. Nicholas Culpeper, herbalist and doctor (a very popular one, they say) is
always slightly suspect: he really did suggest too many uses for
everything. For White-Lillys his summary is 'Poyson, Pestilential
Feavers, Venom, Dropsie, Scald-Heads (?), Unites Sinews, Ulcers,
Afterbirth, Plague-sores, Swellings in the Privities, Burnings,
Scaldings, Hair restoreth.'

Gerard gave more space to the description of the flowers—and
the story of how the plant sprang from some of Juno's milk that
was spilled—but he mentioned that 'the root . . . stamped with
honey gleweth together sinues that be cut in sunder.'

I used to know an old gardener and he used to sing a song
(home-made I think) most of which I have forgotten, and most
of which is better forgotten, but the main theme was that he had
no luck with girls or Lilies.

He grew, if I remember rightly

> 'Potatoes and Strawberries
> And mustard and cress.
> Big Onions and Marrows
> To take home in barrows
> But with girls and with Lilies
> I have no success.'

I believe the song built up to the fact that

> 'I don't care for Lilies
> And for girls even less.'

What he meant was that the Lilies did not care for him. He
could not grow them. And many other gardeners were, and are,
in the same fix.

There are literally hundreds of species and varieties of Lilies.
Many of them are not available to the ordinary gardener; some
are not available to any gardeners. Patrick M. Synge in his *Guide
to Bulbs* describes (I've counted) a hundred and fifty, and a score
or so of hybrids. Again, a lot you could not buy and a lot you

would not want to buy, but subtracting all these you are left with a few score of bulbs from which you can grow some of the most beautiful flowers in the world. So the spring garden crammed with Daffodils and the late spring garden full of Tulips should be followed by the summer garden glorious with Lilies of all sizes, shapes, colours and scents.

And is it?

Never!

I won't elaborate. I merely say look in the next dozen gardens you walk round and count how many flourishing colonies of Lilies you see. You won't need the fingers of even one hand to keep the score!

I am making this quite clear, because in spite of the apologists, except for a dedicated minority of experts, growing Lilies well and keeping them growing well year after year is no easy task.

I love Lilies; I grow them; I recommend all gardeners who love beautiful flowers to grow them. But though I grow and recommend only a dozen or so of the easiest (luckily also the best) I know the risk of disappointment and loss.

Any good Lily bulb of those classified as easy will give a fine head of flowers in its first season. That is the nature of bulbs: they contain the next season's flowers. You can hardly prevent good results. It is making the bulbs produce the same results in subsequent years that is the difficulty, though I must admit that my own garden has a heavy soil that warms slowly and late and I am sure it is not the kind in which Lilies flourish.

There are also inconsistencies. My brother had a flourishing colony of Madonna Lilies in his Pembrokeshire garden. The bulbs were enormous and bore excellent blooms year after year. He gave me some, digging out forkfuls of the bulbs as casually as if they were potatoes. I planted these carefully in a prepared bed in my garden doing all those things that I ought to have done.

I put mortar rubble in the soil because Madonna Lilies are one of the few in the genus that like lime; I chose a warm spot with light warm soil and I gave them 'head in the sun and feet in the shade' that a successful grower told me was essential.

They did very well indeed. They flowered splendidly and went

on doing so for many years. I think my colony increased for I gave
away bulbs to admirers.

But I was like the king in Byron's poem.

> 'He counted them at break of day—
> And when the sun set where were they?'

I think an odd bulb lingers on in that corner but I have not had
a flower for years. What went wrong? Who knows! One of our
more notable winters perhaps.

And I am not alone. I know a cottage by the roadside in a
nearby village and every June there was such a blossoming of
pure whiteness, such a scent in the air . . . yet the other day we
came past the cottage and my wife said, 'Do you remember the
Madonna Lilies in that garden? Where have they gone?' Where
indeed!

One thing that is very wrong indeed is a method of selling the
bulbs. If you buy bulbs from a good bulb merchant or from a
Lily expert, the sort of chap who puts on breath-taking displays
at the Royal Horticultural Society Shows then you are as safe
as you can be. But if you buy them casually at small shops or
worse still, off the stalls at stores, then you are not. Lily bulbs
should never be bought dry and rootless like those of daffodils
and tulips. It is doubtful if they ever completely rest. Those thick
thong-like roots should not be allowed to dry out—or they should
be protected as much as possible from drying and shrivelling.
Thousands of Lily bulbs of the commonest species are sold in the
stores every year. And though they may give a few flowers,
even a few very good flowers, in their first season, many will never
show as much as a leaf afterwards. In what garden will you see
the thriving colonies those bulbs should have become?

Lily bulbs with dried-out roots are invalids.

I am not attacking the stores. Their managers and sales girls are
not expected to be expert gardeners. The stores have done noble
work indeed in making a wide selection of excellent bulbs available to us at moderate prices. They have put colour into tens of
thousands of gardens; pleasure and delight into the hearts of
tens of thousands of gardeners. They have done truly noble work
for our gardens. But Lily bulbs are not improved by lying on open

stalls in warm, sometimes overwarm, shops. It is fatal to them.

The fault lies in those foreign merchants—I understand often in China and Japan—who dig up the bulbs from fields and send them, badly prepared and badly packed, by the shipload. (This, by the way, is what I have been told.) It is the only way of being able to sell the bulbs cheaply. But a bulb that dies is dear at any price.

To be fair to the oriental growers, why should they reverence these bulbs particularly? For thousands of years they have been grown, fields full of them, for food! Imagine it: *Lilium brownii* is an outstanding beauty, not easy to grow, and as I write the price in a catalogue before me is 25s a bulb. While in China it was, still is so far as I know, a common food for peasants. *L. auratum,* again one of the choicest species—a well-grown bulb in flower is enough to take your breath away—is 6s at my merchants. It has been an article of diet in China, Japan and Korea for the last thousand years. One of the American species, *L. pardalinum,* is edible, though whether it is eaten now as it was eaten by the Red Indians I would not know.

So really, Lily culture starts by buying healthy bulbs with healthy roots. And the second stage is to get them planted as soon as possible.

As to growing them, the first step is the preparation of the soil.

Take the site first. It is impossible to draw up a short list of rules that will suit *all* species. But there are a few rules that apply to all the commoner species. Lilies are, generally speaking, plants of light woodland. That means they like a fair amount of light, though not often strong hot sunshine, but they appreciate shade round the roots. Many careful growers plant them among low shrubs: they are often used as companions to Azaleas and Rhododendrons, but there is a risk that those two take the best of the plant food and starve the bulb. That can be rectified by feeding of course. I think often dwarf shrubs are better companions or even some medium height herbaceous plants. Santolina, Lavender, Hypericum and Potentilla are all suitable little shrubs to use. Most Lilies are fairly tall so they will look after the sunlight part. 'Feet in the shade, head in the sun' was a Lily rule given me many years ago by I don't know whom, and it is still quite a good general rule.

A few Lilies tolerate lime but most do not and to a few it is fatal. So if you have not a lime-free soil introduce it—even in raised beds if necessary or forswear the flowers altogether. Lime does wash out of soil, so except in natural lime areas many gardens have very little present (it is easy to test) and the addition of plenty of peat and leaf-mould is sufficient.

The next important point is drainage. There are swamp Lilies, mostly American species, but I think none of these grow in the water itself. They grow a little above the water level so that their roots have free access to unlimited moisture. But all other Lilies, or all the others we are likely to grow, need perfect drainage. After the lime factor I would say this is the most important thing to attend to. Very easy too. Dig in lots and lots of coarse sand and grit. Fine chippings like those used in road-making are good for the job, but you need the sand as well. But—do *not* use sea-sand which contains lime in the form of broken shell, and make sure the grit also is not a limestone grit.

After that it goes without saying that a heavy soil will need thorough preparation and may even require drainage. Double digging (two spade lengths down) will be necessary, and if energy allows full trenching would be better.

As to the soil itself my experience has been that the bulbs are heavy feeders, needing a lot of humus in their soil, but growers often disagree as to the form in which it should be given. Peat is splendid to bring soil to good physical condition but it does not contain a lot of the actual nutriments that plants need, or not in the form in which they can use it. Leaf-mould is excellent but it is not enough to use broken up leaves. The leaves should be completely broken down to a sweet dark brown mould. I have known gardeners (I am among them!) to collect the soil under the dead leaves in oak and beech woods, forgetting that many fibrous tree roots have been feeding on it since it fell. It sounds as if you can't do right! But you can if you try.

A mulch of autumn leaves spread on beds of Lilies (or any beds) is an excellent way of adding food to the soil but it must be done every year and spectacular results must not be expected at once.

Garden compost is good for the Lilies, and soft compost (from quickly rotting material) is ready when about a year old. I have grown them in pure compost with very good results.

Opinions are divided about manure. If you are lucky enough to have a supply my own opinion is that old manure, well rotted, is a grand food. All growers say do not use fresh manure and I agree but mainly, I think, because that is what has been dinned into me for years. I've never tried it and I don't suppose many other gardeners have. But I've put some pretty ripe stuff on the Rose bed in my time, with enough ammonia stink to knock you over. But the Roses, bless 'em, never flinched and by spring everything was wholesome and sweet again. Still I wouldn't chance the fresh hot stuff on the Lilies.

The actual planting of the bulbs is simple enough, but it is important to remember that some of them form roots on the base of the stems while others do not. The former should have soil three or four times the depth of the bulb above them. And when they grow they will need top-dressing with leaf-mould or compost as soon as young roots show on the stem. Bulbs with stems that do not have roots are for shallow planting. A bulb merchant or the catalogues will tell you which are the stem rooters.

If you have a good soil and good bulbs the rest is simple. Every gardener has his own methods, but the plants should not need feeding and they should not need watering. Grown in small colonies in sheltered sites they ought not to need stakes, but tall heavy spires may need the support of a cane in rough weather.

Slugs will eat some species so a few pellets scattered round now and then will lessen the danger.

What protection to use against the scissors of marauding women I have not yet discovered.

Before I describe the few easy species I love to grow let me give my own method of growing them.

I grow them in pots in the greenhouse.

It sounds like defeatism to abandon the drifts among the Rhododendrons, but Lilies are among the easiest and most beautiful pot plants in the world. They give no trouble, you do not miss the display because you cannot get out to look at them in a cold wet spell; the flowers are free of blemishes and weather stains, and, though the bulbs do tend to deteriorate, with care they will flower for many years. There is really no need to go into cultural details. Plant the bulbs whenever they are available; use a compost rich in humus and lots of grit for drainage. Use large but not unwieldy pots, say 8½ inch and you have to use your judgement as to the number of bulbs per pot. I generally put three medium sized *L. regale* but when I can get a really large *L. auratum* I like it growing alone. Leave space for top-dressing stem-roots. I leave my pots under glass from planting to flowering then give them a spell outside. When the leaves dry get as much of the old compost out as possible or repot. Bulbs with fresh soil to feed on will last longer than those that stay in the same compost year after year, and there is a danger of overlooking them when you are busy over so many other things in summer.

Strange to say, I had no lasting success in growing them in the raised beds I have in my greenhouse (though Arum Lilies, which are not Lilies, flourish in them). Possibly there was lime present washed down from shaded glass or whitewashed sash-bars. But in tubs the flowers are excellent, and tubs of Lilies grown under glass are fine for carrying out to porch or paved garden.

I will give a short description of the Lilies I grow myself and like best (which does not mean I *always* have all of them all the time). But these I am familiar with and can recommend. If you become ambitious to try more of these wonderful flowers, get a catalogue from one of the specialists. There you will find beauties enough to keep anyone satisfied for a lifetime. And of course join the Lily Society (affiliated to the Royal Horticultural Society), exhibit your best blooms, and, if you happen to be a dustman you can triumph over a duke; or if you are a duke, you can put the dustman's nose out of joint. There are no social distinctions among Lily growers.

I have seen from time to time excellent colonies of first-rate Lilies in one place or another, but like the Madonnas I mentioned earlier they seem to come and go. The only Lily I have found growing with complete freedom and great lustiness as if they were permanent is *L. pyrenaicum.* They grow in a few farmhouse gardens in the most bleak unpromising hillsides in Radnorshire, great bulbs as big as breakfast cups that flower with the greatest freedom year after year. This Lily is not very common and the bulbs are not very cheap and the gardens where they grow are not noted for many flowers or choice flowers. The people call them 'Turn-around-Gentleman' and at close quarters they smell horrid. They are bright yellow with black markings and reddish anthers. How they come to be growing where they are is a minor mystery. A few bulbs stolen from, or thrown out of, the Hall garden, maybe?

Or did some Spanish nobleman, escaping from a wrecked Armada galleon, fill his pockets with some bulbs to eat? And then at a hospitable Welsh farmhouse throw them away outside the door. And did he marry the farmer's daughter, to start that black-haired, dark-eyed type of face you meet sometimes among the hills . . .

No, that's not a theory. I'm being romantic!

About 1935 or 1936 I got hold of a Lily specialist's catalogue. I still have it. I know the year because it is printed on the cover, 1935-36. It is not so much a catalogue as a text book, and a text book with very fine illustrations into the bargain. All sorts of information is given about the species listed and I fell completely under the enchantment of Lilies. I was fairly set to become a Lily gardener and only one thing stopped me: I had very little money to spare. The prices were not high; in fact they were ridiculously low compared with those of today. But then salaries were ridiculously low compared with those of today.

In a good recent Lily catalogue I find *L. auratum virginale* is 30s. In my old catalogue I see it listed at 5s. But 5s was a lot of money in those days when one's daily ration of cigarettes was 6d. *L. brownii* was 3s 6d.; it is (in the latest catalogue) 25s. 3s 6d. was dear thirty years ago; 25s is dear today. We get more money in our pocket and the prices go up!

Anyhow, I just could not afford many Lily bulbs, and sometimes I could not afford any at all, while the rarities I could not manage at any time. So, as a specialist I never really got started.

Out of the hundreds of species that were available, ambition yielded to finance. But the few I did manage (I don't think I ever

Eranthis hyemalis: the yellow flowers appear in and January and February

Double Snowdrops
come out in
February in sheltered
places

Above: Snowdrops growing in a wood at St Ishmaels in Pembrokeshire
Below: Crocuses in full flower round the bole of a tree

A field of Daffodils at Hoogmade in Holland

The Hyacinth is an easy and decorative bulb for a pot

Daffodils in the Keukenhof at Lisse in Holland

grew them all at once) were as beautiful as any of the unattainable ones.

Lilium auratum was one of my favourites. The worst of describing these flowers is that each species seems to be your favourite until you remember another you grew that is equally lovely. So I'll say right away that my three favourites out of all I've grown or seen are *L. auratum, L. regale* and *L. speciosum.* Next I think comes the Madonna Lily *L. candidum* and the Easter Lily *L. longiflorum formosum.* After these there is a group of bulbs that I have found easy and which in most cases have gone on flowering in my garden for many years. They are *L. croceum,* generally known as the Orange Lily, *L. hansoni, L. henryi, L. martagon,* Turk's cap, *L. pyrenaicum, L. tigrinum,* the Tiger Lily, and *L. umbellatum,* which may now be listed as *L. dauricum.*

I find I have listed a dozen and they would make a very good start for any beginner, perhaps also for a few who are not beginners. To describe individual flowers is no easy task. I suppose you could say one Lily is very like another Lily of the same colour. It is not, only we lack the words to distinguish them.

L. auratum is a Japanese species that was introduced by Veitch in 1862. The flower is white with, in most varieties, a golden stripe down each petal. Many flowers are borne on each stem and they can be up to six or seven inches across. Most Lilies are good but this is really outstanding. Given good drainage it does not seem particular as to soil, yet it is not easy to establish in the garden.

L. brownii is not on my list but is added here as it is a very choice flower indeed, in fact is one of the finest and most fragrant of the race.

L. candidum is familiar to most people. The petals are snow-white and the scent is rich and strong. The usual advice is to plant in a gravelly type of soil containing plenty of mortar rubble.

L. croceum is the Orange Lily, one of the easy species and not at all difficult to establish. As long as the drainage is good it is said to do well in heavy soils but I think it is safest with *all* Lilies to have one that has a lot of humus in it.

L. giganteum is another well-known species I have not grown. It is for woodlands and the bulb needs shallow planting. In favourable circumstances it will grow 10 to 12 feet tall. I was ambitious to have a few bulbs, but then I saw it in flower at Wisley and decided it was, for me, a curiosity rather than a flower I wanted.

L. hansoni. This is said to be dependable but I have not had any great success with it. I have a suspicion that my bulbs were not very healthy. The flowers are spotted orange-yellow.

L. henryi. This seems a very easy one and not hard to establish in light shade. The stems are tall, generally about five feet. The orange flowers are borne in large numbers on each stem.

L. martagon is the Turk's Cap—which gives the shape of the flower—an old species, mostly in wine or reddish shades. It is quite easy. There is a white form which is very good.

L. pyrenaicum. The yellow black-spotted flowers are pretty but the scent sometimes tolerable at a distance, is rather formidable in large doses. In my last garden in light and rather poor soil it grew and spread and formed enormous bulbs. In my present garden with colder, heavier more fertile soil, it just keeps alive but seldom flowers.

L. regale. This popular Lily was introduced by E. H. Wilson at the beginning of the century. Unfortunately one runs out of superlatives but gardeners really did get excited about it. It appeared also that it was going to be easy to grow, doing well on almost any soil and being tolerant of lime. Well, it was not so easy as all that! Millions of bulbs have been planted and the flower should be as common in summer as the daffodil is in spring. Some of the failures are due to poor cultivation, some to the wrong soil and very many, I suspect, to faulty drainage. But most, I'd guess, failed to make it because they were dead from the bulb down. It cannot be stressed too much that a Lily with dead or shrivelled roots stands a very poor chance indeed.

E. H. Wilson, who discovered the flower on the banks of the Min River, a tributary of the Yangtse, did see them flowering as freely as we would like to. There in June by the wayside, in rock crevices, by the torrent's edge, and high up on the mountainside and precipice, this Lily in full bloom greets the weary wayfarer not in twos and threes but in hundreds and thousands—aye, in tens of thousands. Their slender stems, each from 2 to 4 feet tall, flexible and tense as steel, overtop the coarse grasses and scrub, each crowned with one to several large funnel-shaped flowers, more or less wine coloured without, clear canary yellow within the tube, and each stamen filament tipped with a golden anther.'

I don't suppose even the most thoughtful of us realises how much we owe to the plant collectors. Of course such a job must be full of interest but it is and was not all beer and skittles. Wilson went back to the Min in 1910 to get more bulbs and had his left leg broken in two places by falling rock. Pretty bad fractures, for it was touch and go as to whether the leg would have to be amputated. I'm told he limped for the rest of his life.

And, by the way, a growing tip from Wilson himself. He warned growers not to 'ruin its constitution with rich food'.

L. speciosum is another of my great favourites. I suppose I have indicated about auratum and regale that they are unbeatable, so I must be careful what I say. But I remember my first bulb grown many, many years ago, *L. speciosum rubrum*, I think, and I grew it in a large pot and when it flowered I really was enchanted: 'all rugged with rubies and garnets and sparkling with crystal points.'

There are a lot of species and garden forms available but *L. speciosum album* and *L. speciosum rubrum* take some beating.

L. tigrinum is the Tiger Lily. It arrived here about 1804 but had been grown as a field crop in the Far East for unknown centuries, not for the flowers but for food. I don't know who gave it its name because as one author has remarked, red tigers with purple spots cannot have been very common anywhere. Yellow and orange are colours we do not lack in the garden so perhaps that is why it is not more popular. It is a very easy plant to grow and colonies thrive and even increase in some gardens. I have a feeling it does better in harsh dry soil than in a rich one. Propagation is easy because bulbs form in the leaf axils and they fall to the ground and quickly take root. It is a good idea to gather these and grow them by themselves until they are large enough to plant out. It might be mentioned here that Lily propagation is by seed, by growing single scales much as one would grow cuttings and by division of bulbs. All are theoretically easy but seedlings and the bulbs formed by scales need practice.

L. umbellatum (*L. dauricum*) is another fairly easy species. It has orange or yellow flowers. A group of these will make a fine splash of colour in the border or they can be grown among low shrubs.

A lot of work has been done hybridising Lilies in recent years. I have not grown any of these hybrids in my own garden but there are certainly some magnificent and brilliant flowers available. I'm afraid I am a tiny bit conservative about Lilies and rate the species so highly that I do not value new introductions as I should. And I am not sure how easy to cultivate the new-comers will be. I hope they will be easier than some of their parents and then we shall have a great flowering of Lilies every-where as they become popular (and, we hope, cheaper).

The Lilies of the Field which Jesus mentioned were Anemones, someone told me. Why on earth should they be? Lilies grow wild in the Near East as well as the Far East. In fact someone brought me a few bulbs from Cyprus and I flowered them—though I have no idea what species they were. They had long pure white trum-pets with a delicious scent. I'm tired of having all our little beliefs debunked. 'Behold the Anemones of the field.' No, no, Solomon was as handsome as *those* in his glory; they were Lilies.

And what of the golden Lilies of France, the Fleur-de-Lis? Well, those, believe it or not, were originally toads. They were the three black toads (*crapauds*) the device of Clovis, King of the Franks. An angel gave a hermit a beautiful azure shield on which three gold Lilies shone like jewels. The hermit gave it to Queen Clotilde who gave it to Clovis. After that he won all bat-tles over his enemies, so he adopted the Lilies as his device, and they became the badge of France.

A Lily is a much more romantic symbol than a toad, though the nickname Johnny Crapaud stuck to Frenchmen through a few centuries.

Chapter 3: THE DAISY FAMILY

The Daisy family is the largest of the dicotyledons. They 'are easily recognised by their characteristic inflorescence, which consists of numerous small flowers packed together into a head and surrounded by one or more rows of involucral bracts or phyllaries. The individual florets may be zygomorphic with an elongate strap-shaped, or ligulate, corolla, or they may be regular with a tubula corolla cleft at the apex into five short lobes.'

So now you know.

After that—how far apart the botanist and the gardener dwell —I may be forgiven if I explain that dicotyledons are plants that start their lives with two seed leaves (grasses are monocotyledons) and those who know the word will excuse me if I introduce the word *genus* of which the plural is *genera*. The genera are the separate kinds, Daisies, Sunflowers, Dahlias, Asters and so on. The point is that the Daisy family contains more than 900 of these genera. Each genus contains separate species, *Aster alpinus, Aster amellus, Aster multiflorum* and all the other Asters. And each species contains named garden kinds—think of how many named Dahlias there are—so taking one thing with another the entire family must contain tens of thousands.

A host indeed; luckily in the garden we are concerned only with a selection, but it is a most important selection and of the greatest importance to gardeners. If all the Daisy-type plants were subtracted from us the garden would be a very poverty-stricken place. I have heard the criticism that too many disport themselves in yellow flowers and we are rich in yellow anyhow, but when we think of Dahlias and annual Asters (more correctly *Calistephus*) we must not take that too seriously.

THE DAHLIA

Years ago when I was writing my first book about gardening—
or more perhaps about gardens and gardeners—I hunted out the
story of the Dahlia. And this is what I found.

The plant is a native of Mexico, and our own garden varieties
have descended from one species, *Dahlia variabilis* which in the
wild state is a tall untidy bushy plant with purplish flowers of no
great distinction. But it sports readily, and that is why we have
the rainbow of shades that dazzles you from every cottage garden and park every summer.

It was first described under its native name of Acoctii by
Francesco Hernandez, physician to Philip II of Spain. He had
gone to Mexico to study the cochineal insect which lived on
cacti and from which the well-known scarlet dyes were made.
The plant was next mentioned in 1787 by a Frenchman named
Menonville and two years later seeds and plants were sent to Eu-
rope by Abbé Cavinelles, the Director of the Royal Gardens in
Madrid. At the same time he sent some to a Swedish botanist,
André Dahl, from whom the plant got its botanical name.

About this time the Ambassador to the Spanish Court was the
Marquis of Bute and he got hold of some seeds of the Acoctii
plant—it was not yet the Dahlia—and Lady Bute sent them home
and some of the seeds reached Kew.

The gardeners at Kew grew the plants with enthusiasm realis-
ing they were on to something good. But clever people are not
always wise; they kept them perpetually in flower not understanding that the roots needed a period of complete rest. As a
result they all died.

Fortunately André Dahl had either more consideration or more
sense (or both!) so the European stock was not completely lost.
But it was about fourteen years later before it was brought to
England again, and again it was a woman, Lady Holland, who
sent seeds from Madrid to Buonaiuti, her husband's librarian.

You can't keep a good man down, they say, and presumably
the same can be said for a good flower, but it is to those
two women, Lady Bute and Lady Holland that we owe all our
lovely Dahlias.

The flower did not become popular very quickly. The Empress Josephine grew it at Malmaison and many French varieties were brought to Britain when the Wars came to an end. Hogg, the well-known Paddington nurseryman considered it too large for small gardens, but others thought differently because John Wedgewood, one of the founders of the Royal Horticultural Society was growing two hundred varieties by 1835. But from what literature is available I think it was many years before it became popular with the man-in-the-street gardener. The Dahlia Society was started in 1880.

Nowadays we have a lot of different types of Dahlias from large to tiny, from dwarf to six-footers. There is a story that Cactus Dahlias descended from a single tuber which was the only survivor from a lot sent from Mexico. If that is true it is only in keeping with the almost haphazard way the flower has got into our gardens. There are thousands of garden varieties in all shades from the quiet to the barbaric. Most people seem to buy dry tubers in spring and just plant them out in the garden. Whether these are saved to flower another year is anybody's guess and mine is that a lot are left out. Some will survive; many will not.

When I started gardening there was a definite routine in Dahlia growing which everyone seemed to follow carefully. Starting with the dormant tubers in spring the first thing was to put these on a tray or in a shallow box, cover with light soil and water them. In a week or two, shoots appeared and as soon as they were big enough to handle they were taken off, with or without a wedge of the old tuber and rooted as cuttings. Each cutting made a strong young plant and each plant was set out in the beds in June or whenever frost danger was over (if it ever is in our climate). There was a theory that new plants from cuttings were more robust than what you got by planting the old tubers.

In the autumn when flowering was over tubers were dug up, stored dry or near dry in a box or under the greenhouse staging, and you were ready to start all over again next spring.

Of course, it is easier to take a dry tuber from a polythene bag or out of a box with a gay picture on it, and it is less work to buy a new supply each spring than to root cuttings—but I don't think it is as much fun. After all a lot of the joy of gardening is doing things and you get a kick out of raising your own new plants.

The actual culture was, and is, very simple. Dahlias love a deep rich soil full of rotted manure and/or compost. They appreciate drainage but must have plenty of moisture. You must support the tall ones and if you want large flowers each stem must be thinned to one bud. If you want the real monsters the size of dinner plates you must buy tubers or plants of the correct varieties (often marked G for gigantic in the catalogues) disbud very thoroughly and feed them with liquid manure. There is a yarn that they enjoy a sugar solution but I never got round to trying it. Anyhow, they grow big enough without sugar. It's as easy as eating your dinner as our roadman used to say.

I should think the only man to rejoice when the Dahlias were over was Mr Jorrocks: 'Hurrah! blister my kidneys,' exclaimed he in delight, 'it is a frost!—the dahlias are dead!' So hunting could start!

It wouldn't matter only there is always a host of buds still to come out. I tried lifting tubers and replanting them in a bed in the greenhouse when frost time is near. Sure enough it worked. Lifted with a good ball of soil the plants hardly flag, all the unopened buds come out, and we have a very nice show of flowers well into November. Then, as if they realise the time to rest has come, they cease to produce any more buds and the plants die.

I have kept Dahlia tubers alive in the garden by tipping a bucket of ashes or sand over each plant in autumn. The only drawback to this is that in warm gardens the plants start too early the following year and the frost nips them; or they come so late that summer is nearly over before they flower.

And slugs love them!

I have not tried tasting the tubers, but I have been told they are bitter. Mexicans have used them as a tonic. A drug called inulin has been extracted from them.

There is a plant with a similar name. It is Dalea, named after a botanist Dr Samual Dale. To avoid confusion it was suggested that Dahlia should become Georgia after the botanist Georgi. It did not catch on though the name Georgine has been used occasionally on the Continent.

THE BEST DAISY: CHRYSANTHEMUM

I am sure that gardeners grow more Dahlias than they do Chrysanthemums. I am equally sure that the latter is a better flower and I think ninety per cent of gardeners agree with me. And having said that I realise I do not know why. The Dahlia has no scent, but apart from that it is doubtful if, in good looks and general beauty and handsomeness of plant there is much to choose between the two. But there is no reasonableness about choosing a flower or a wife (or husband). The wind bloweth where it listeth.

In our country the flower has not a very long history. As with many flowers later to become popular it appeared, disappeared, appeared again, was cultivated without any great enthusiasm at Kew and by a few growers. Then someone gets keen, improves cultivation, breeds, selects, discards and selects again and suddenly the great body of gardeners realise that the Ugly Duckling is a Swan.

The first plants in Europe were grown in Holland, but Bregaius, the botanist who grew them, did not raise any enthusiasm even among the canny Dutch gardeners who generally had and still have a keen eye for a lovely flower or a good commercial proposition. It was about a century later, 1795, that some plants reached Kew from France. Still no excitement. New varieties arrived from China and very very slowly a little interest was awakened. A Society was formed in Norwich in 1829 and others soon after in Birmingham and Swansea. Then in 1846 a number of growers at Stoke Newington formed what was later to become the National Chrysanthemum Society and we can say that then the flower was launched on its career.

Many men did their share in advancing the fortunes of the Chrysanthemum. A grower by the name of John Salter raised many improved varieties and the plant collector, Robert Fortune brought new ones from China and Japan. To Fortune we owe the Japanese variety from which our Large Exhibition class is descended.

In the Far East the story is very different. The flower has been famous there for thousands of years. Confucius mentioned it in

500 B.C. From China the flower was introduced to Japan and apparently became the favourite of royalty for it became the personal emblem of the Mikado and one of the Emperors wrote poetry in its praise. Only royalty and the nobility were allowed to grow it and the Order of the Chrysanthemum was instituted. Incidentally the Japanese flag is not the Rising Sun but a Chrysanthemum. The Japanese practically canonised the flower: it was left to the Chinese to discover that the petals are edible and to grow flowers specially as additions to the salad bowl.

Our herbalists, in the Golden Age of Herbs, had no Chrysanthemums to toy with, but you cannot help wondering what they would have made of a plant with such a strong persistent fragrance, which, by the way, is as strong in the leaves as in the flowers, and as strong in dead dried petals as in live ones. The nearest they had was Featherfew or Feverfew with its golden leaves, bright little Daisy flowers and pungent smell.

Of course the recipes of herbalists of old times are rather amusing, but considering the concoctions a good advertisement can persuade us to pour into our insides we really should not poke fun. A lot of people and a lot of doctors have never heard of a hop pillow, but a pillow stuffed with hops will (usually) ensure a night's sleep more sound than will all those millions of sleeping pills prescribed so freely. And, on the more serious side, though a delicate patient or two might have died through taking, say too much Foxglove Tea, no herbalist that I ever heard of ever prescribed anything as disastrous as thalidomide.

According to Wordsworth a Primrose by the river's brim, to Peter Bell a yellow Primrose was to him and it was nothing more but garden flowers are in a different category altogether. Roses, Lilies, Daffodils, Tulips, the breeder gets to work on them, the classless society vanishes and we are offered a score of different kinds. Either you pick your favourite or you may end up by growing in all its different forms one flower only. And that would be a sad fate.

The Chrysanthemum, like all the other aristocrats of the flower world is another house divided. I can count ten different types in a catalogue I have picked up. No doubt I missed a few. And this is complicated by the fact that some of them are sub-divided

into early ones and late ones. It is complicated still further by
the fact that skilled growers have worked out methods by which
the plants can be coaxed into flower at any time of the year. I
prefer to ignore that. The business of growing flowers out of season is getting too complicated for me. I know I shall be right out-
of-date soon but I enjoy my flowers in season.

So to me the Chrysanthemum is the flower of autumn. It
comes, if left alone, from late summer to December. That I
would say is a fair length of time to enjoy them and from about
January onwards I look forward to Snowdrops, Crocuses, Daffodils, Tulips. As for types I simplify them: the early ones are for
outdoors and will bloom when most of the summer flowers are
finishing. Then come the decoratives in October and November
with some late varieties managing to hold on until Christmas.
Once I grew the monster, mop-headed beauties sometimes
called Japanese, sometimes Large Decoratives but they were
hard work and I have renounced them in favour of the easier
plants.

If you want a wider choice there are Singles, Pompoms, Cas-
cade, Charm, Korean, Quill Petalled and others. Culture of any
is basically simple and the same for all (except for the enormous
show flowers) and this in reality boils down to good soil and lov-
ing care. But the experts have made growing Exhibition flowers
a formidable and lengthy task. J. H. Goddard in *Chrysanthemum
Growers' Treasury* makes it sound almost terrifying: '. . . if the
"mops" are to maintain their prestige as the hybridisers intended
they should, there is only one way—that is super-culture. They
demand every possible help in the way of soils, manures, fertilisers, watering and cleanliness. They "scream" for the right size
pots, the canes they lean against, the constant picking of side
growths, potting just as they need potting and not before, and
pinching at the appropriate date in order that the buds come to
time so that they may develop in the dewy nights.'

Mr Goddard even suggests that you should speak to them before leaving them for the night 'to inquire of them, "Are you comfortable?" or, "Is there anything more I can do?".'

Being funny, of course: but the grower, slowly going out of

his mind would have a shock if one of them said, 'Yes, clear out and shut that door!'

I have grown the big ones, as I said, but I was not doing it for the shows so there were often compromises with the rule-book. I think it is worth while if only because one learns a lot in that way. The flowers, with any luck at all are gorgeous. After you have done it a few times either you want to go on growing them or you do not. I did not.

While I am on the subject I consider it worth while giving any plants what Mr Goddard calls 'super-culture'. In my early gardening days I did just that. The results on the whole did my morale a lot of good but much more important I learned all about the flowers, fruit and vegetables I selected. Then would come the day when I realised that all is vanity and I was not absolutely bound to enslave myself and my family to a plant and I would be content with more modest results. But I did know what to do to get those at their best, and I understood very well what could be left out and what could not.

So my Chrysanthemums no longer took the breath away or sent visiting gardeners away eating their hearts out in envy. I suppose they were, and are, about as good as you would see in a not-too-expensive florist's window. They give the greenhouse colour in autumn and are delightful in vases.

Early Chrysanthemums will flower out-of-doors. You buy or beg or raise from your plants cuttings in early spring, plant them in good large groups (if you have enough plants) when the soil has warmed up, and with a minimum of attention have very nice flowers from August. They do not always give of their best on clay, but prefer light warm soil which has been enriched with good manure, or compost, or fertilisers.

In gardens in the south, where the soil suits them, some of the later decoratives will flourish in a sunny border and may be laden with blooms as late as Christmas. I have seen them grow in favoured spots in Pembrokeshire, in Essex, and in Hampshire. But in colder places it might not be worth even trying.

For growing under glass the very simplest method I have seen consists of getting good strong young plants in spring and planting them outside in a warm border. They will need stakes or ty-

ing to wires as they grow: a Chrysanthemum plant that has
fallen over and been allowed to grow crookedly is a pitiable
sight. About mid-September or October the plants are lifted carefully (the soil clings to the roots nicely on a wet day!) and replanted in a greenhouse border. They can be potted if this
is preferred. They may flag for a day or two but soon recover.
They can be given a little weak liquid fertiliser, and I think they
make a better show if they are disbudded to one bud per stem. I
have grown the plants and used this method but nowadays I take
a little more trouble, though I don't suppose the end result
is much better, but spring in my district is often cold, Charles
Kingsley's 'brave north-easter' shrivels up everything in sight and
the plants have to stay under glass.

So I plant all my cuttings in 8 or 9 inch pots (forget the Show
technique of moving always from one size pot to one size larger)
water sparingly to avoid wet sour soil, put one or two stakes per
plant. When the weather becomes more genial the pots stand in
the open. The icy north-easter has been turned to a vicious south-
wester that maliciously flattens everything in its path so I try for
shelter. (My neighbour swears that his Peonies in full bloom is
the signal for the first summer gale!) I give weak liquid manure
once a week all the time.

The only other cultivation is stopping. In growing for shows
this is one of the most difficult skills to learn, because different
varieties have to be stopped at different times, also some flowers
are better on the second lot of shoots than they are on the first,
some are better on the third.

I stop, that is pinch out the growing tips, of all shoots about
mid-April. The plants send out side shoots, and these I stop some
time in summer, say early July.

This seemingly casual treatment, I expect, would fill any of the
Exhibition lads with horror.

But it works!

If my original cutting gave three good stems after the spring
stopping, and they give three more after the summer stopping
then I have a plant that will produce nine lovely Chrysanthemums. What more could a gardener ask!

Individual flowers come in a wide variety: some shaggy, some neatly incurved and the Rayonante class with their quilled petals is most attractive. There are some lovely singles, large and small, in the family. The big ones when well grown can be gorgeous. But the small singles are equally good. They will, if treated with care, make little bushes absolutely covered with flowers. One plant will do very well in, say, a 7 inch pot, but a more impressive show is achieved by planting three small plants near the edge of a 9 inch pot. That does make an eyeful. I remember growing a group like this once and I brought it into the house and passed it off on my friends as one plant. Cheating? Not a bit of it. Why should fishermen have all the best lies?*

A few classes of dwarf plants have been developed in recent years. These are good in the border but are really a gift to people who must have their gardens in confined spaces such as window boxes or jardinieres. Of course they are lovely for rooms. Of the dwarf variety, the little pom-poms are very attractive, and they are so completely easy that, once cuttings are put in their pots, they need no attention at all.

The worst of gossiping about any one flower whether verbally or on paper is that you go on and on . . . and on . . .

Or I do.

I have spent too long on this incomparable Daisy so in the words of the old song:

'Saddle and bridle, they lie on the shelf,
If you want any more you must sing it yourself.'

And the tune you shall sing? Well, write to any good Chrysanthemum specialist for his catalogue. You'll find music enough in that.

A lot of the people in our village called the flowers 'Mums'. Many could not pronounce Chrysanthemums; I doubt if any could spell it.

I remember our blacksmith, eighty years old if he was a day, showing the new parson round his garden.

He pointed to a row of fine, tall, staked plants.

* He (the Rev. Rowland Hill) did not see any reason why the devil should have all the good tunes.

'Them's my Mums,' he said proudly.

The parson took a good look at him to make sure it wasn't a joke.

'My word!' he said. 'She must be a great age.'

The earliest Daisy in flower in my garden is the Doronicum. It has rather coarse leaves and stems, and deep yellow Sunflower blossoms on 2 foot stems from early spring until June. Some gardeners affect to despise it, but to me it is always welcome, the groups I have making cheerful patches of colour under the often grey skies of spring. It seems to seed itself freely and I get fresh colonies here and there, but the best of them grow under an apple tree in company with a horde of Honesty and the yellow-purple mixture is really lovely.

It is so easy, as I say, that it grows of itself and all it seems to ask is soil of *some* sort. A plant, free-flowering, pretty and so undemanding of time and trouble should be sure of a welcome anywhere. I would not be without it.

It is a good idea when planting Doronicums to take a little trouble to grow it in the best spot. I don't think soil or aspect matter a lot. It likes the sun because the flower has this peculiarity that it always faces the sun—that is the flower actually moves slightly through the day in order to do so. Apart from that I would not be surprised if it would do well in shade; it certainly grows under trees, flowering before they come into leaf. But being early, the flowers, except for an odd laggard or two, are gone by midsummer. The fading stems have no great attraction so should be hidden by one of the late-comers. In short, plant at or near the back of the border or between late-flowering shrubs.

The common name is Leopard's Bane. This is probably due to some confusion arising when the naming of plants was a more haphazard affair than it is today. The point is that some of the herbalists believed it was the Aconite of the ancient writers. That was poisonous: 'Aconit that baneth or killeth Panthers.' But was

it? Aconite or Monkshood is very poisonous. I've grown it but I
do not think I would today. Gerard considered Doronicum was
Aconite, calling it Wolfes-Bane, and he drew attention to the
poisonous qualities, it '. . . is thought to bee the strongest and
next unto *Thora* in his poisoning qualitie, of all the rest of the
Aconites, or Wolfes banes.'

But some of the early botanists considered it was a herbal plant
which Arab doctors called Dorongi, a very useful herb with no
poisonous qualities at all.

I believe that is probably the truth but even now apparently
there is still some doubt. I have no intention of trying to prove it
is not poisonous, but apparently some of the early botanists have
eaten it and found it to be harmless: a concoction made from the
roots was 'verie pleasant in taste, and verie comfortable.' But the
botanist Mathiolus (after whom the Night Scented Stock, *Mathiolus biconis*, and other stocks, are named) tried it on a dog and
the dog died!

The last of the Daisies to flower is the Sunflower. The common
single Sunflower of the border is *Helianthus decapitalus*, an easy,
cheerful sort of flower that blossoms freely on tall stems through
late summer into autumn. There are some improved garden
forms and at least one double that is useful, pretty and rather
more choice than the type. I have grown it for many years: it is
one of those plants that, once introduced, is not easy to be free of.
Not that I want to be completely without it, but like a friendly
mongrel dog it is very persistent. At various times I have tried to
exile it to out-of-the-way corners of the garden, but it springs
from a mass of tough creeping roots (rhizomes) and it is difficult to get them all out. Every bit that is left starts a healthy new
plant and in a couple of seasons you find you have as many Sunflowers in the borders as you ever had. It would not matter so
much but like a fat man it takes up more than its fair share
of the bed.

The Italian name for Sunflower was girosole, and when another variety with edible roots was introduced about 1604 the
name was corrupted to Jerusalem Artichoke. That seldom bears
flowers in this country and as far as I am concerned the rhizome

as a food is an acquired taste—and I have not acquired it, though many people have.

All the Sunflowers came from America and all were overshadowed by *H. Annuus,* the giant annual Sunflower. It was, in many of the ancient American civilisations, treated with great reverence as the emblem of the Sun God. While it was still a novelty it was regarded with almost as much wonder in Europe where it arrived at the end of the sixteenth century. Gerard said it had grown to a height of 14 feet in his garden, 'where one floure was in weight three pound and two ounces, & crosse overthwart the floure by measure sixteen inches broad'. He found it to be edible too: 'we have found by triall, that the buds before they be floured boiled and eaten with butter, vinegar, and pepper, after the manner of Artichokes are exceedingly pleasant meat.'

Whether that was, and is, correct or not the oil from the seeds is said to have a taste of turpentine and both Parkinson and John Evelyn found the flavour too strong. But the plant has quite a high commercial value. The Indians made a yellow dye from the petals; the pith is very light and has been used as a filling for life-jackets; the leaves are appreciated as food for geese, while the seeds have been used for food for poultry and other birds, while the oil in them has had many uses from making margarine and artists' colours to inclusion in various foods. They are good for teeth, and races who habitually chew them (rather than sweets) suffer very little from tooth decay.

Altogether a very useful plant and, I believe, still an important field crop in a number of countries.

But, in spite of the wonderful pictures of Van Gogh, the annual Sunflower is no longer a favourite with gardeners. Presumably enough is enough, but too much is a joke. Except for an old plant in a rough corner or as a marvel for children's gardens you will search far before you see one of those great round yellow faces staring down at you.

Chapter 5: THE REST OF THE FAMILY

Oh dear! I start thinking of which other Daisies I should include and I find there is almost no end to the list. The Daisies demand not a few chapters but a volume all to themselves. They seem to be crying out from all directions . . . 'Me . . . and me . . . and me . . .' It is a job to be selective when there are so many; I'm like a man in a lifeboat in which there is room for ten off the sinking ship but a hundred clamouring to come in.

Ah well, I started this. I'll have to do the best I can. The one useful factor is that all of them are not too particular about soil and they do not demand a great deal of cultivation. Come to think of it this goes for most good flowering plants, with the exception of a few that need special conditions (Orchids for example) and some tender ones that find our climate and frosts detestable.

It does not do for the garden writer to make everything sound too easy or he will be out of a job, but probably as much as mine tenths of what we grow will give good results without advice from anybody if planted in good well-cultivated soil that contains plenty of the best plant foods. Of all factors that affect plant growth, good soil is essential. A few such as Rhododendrons and Heathers will not grow where there is lime and stone fruit on the other hand needs it. For the rest it must be well dug and well fertilised. And there must be ample moisture. But we seldom fail to have plenty of that.

All the plants I shall describe in this chapter are the easy going creatures that you can plant and forget—until you see them in flower. They are like our roadman says of brands of beer. 'Some's better than others but there's no bad 'uns.'

The Aster is probably the most useful and the most widely-grown member of the tribe. It is best known under its title of Michaelmas Daisy, but Aster it is botanically and under that title you must look it up in the reference books and in the best catalogues. The annual Asters proper name is *Calistephus*. Originally the Michaelmas Daisy was known as Starworts or as Asters; the new name came into use in the 18th century, when Pope Gregory's new calendar came into use, which brought the plant into flower about Michaelmas Day. The first of the family was a little Starwort which came from Italy about the end of the 16th century but there was also a native Starwort which Gerard referred to as Serapia's Turbith. The main body of them were brought from America in the early sixteen hundreds, mainly by one of the Tradescants who were the great gardeners and introducers of new plants in those times. One of the chief classes Novibelgiae gets its name from the Dutch colony—as the New York area was then—of the New Netherlands. Nobody seems to have been very much impressed, and indeed the poorest members of the family are ordinary except as to height, but eventually somebody took a fancy to them and first the Victorian William Robinson and later Ernest Ballard got to work and produced the magnificent plants and very beautiful flowers we have to choose from today.

Did I say all plants need is soil and water? I suppose it was and is the truth but if you give Michaelmas Daisy no more care the results will not be very satisfactory.

Most gardeners spare room for a few clumps in the mixed border and that is all right where there is not very much room. To see them at their best I think they are better grown by themselves. I took all mine out from the scattered spots where they were and planted them in a long narrow border about 18 inches wide. You could call it a sort of hedge, but if there had been room to spare I think I should have had the border twice as wide. This border ran along the length of a path and on the other side there was grass. Michaelmas Daisies like a fairly rich diet so plenty of compost and, when it was available, manure was given.

The one attention these plants must have is efficient staking. If they are grown in clumps or groups and the site is not too windy a piece of string tied round the group is often all they need.

Where there is much wind, though they really should never be planted in windy places, then they need very efficient staking. You can give them this by enclosing the plants while young with a circle of strong pea sticks and allowing the plants to grow through them. Otherwise a number of canes and string going round are called for. If the plants are in a border a good method is to put in strong stakes each side of the row, run wires the whole length, both sides, and run some of these wires from front to back as well. This takes some time to put in but the point is that once set up such a framework will last for many years and you can forget it. All you have to do is to trim away and dispose of the dead stems in late autumn or early spring.

Of course these plants do increase at a merry pace and the counsel of perfection is to lift them every third year and replant a few of the best outer shoots. In practise I found that as long as I was generous with a good fertiliser in autumn they gave good results over a very long time. One tends to forget time in a garden and something you think you put in the year before last turns out to have been there for the last ten years.

My own first Michaelmas Daisy border I'm sure must have been in as long as that before it began to look shabby. Looking at it down the long path when it was in full bloom was one of the best views of the garden in spite of the fact that winter was getting near.

There is now a race of dwarf Michaelmas Daisies. They were bred after the first World War for use in the war cemeteries. They are very compact and free-flowering and though not uncommon are not, I think, as widely known or grown as they deserve.

There are a few very good Asters growing in mountainous country and of course as befits them they are small plants though not so small as to be almost invisible. Also they are easy and decorative. And you are not *bound* to have a rock garden in order to grow rock plants, or Alpines. *Aster alpinus* seems to describe itself by its name. It has lovely flowers and a drift of it will give a good show in any warm, sunny, well-drained spot. A. *thompsonii* is in some ways better for it flowers from August well into the autumn. A. *pappei* comes from South Africa so it is not hardy enough for many gardens but I have heard of almost legendary sky-blue masses in Devonshire and other favoured localities where it has gone on for years. Worth a try anywhere in the southern half of the country.

CALLISTEPHUS

And now, while we are Aster-minded, let us clear up the Great Aster Mystery. The plant most people think of when Aster is mentioned is the Annual Aster, or China Aster because it was brought from China to France in 1728. The true name of this flower is Callistephus, and, if you would like to know (I'm going to tell you anyhow!) is derived from *kallistos* (most beautiful) and *stephos* (a crown).

Not that I am the least bit pedantic about such labels. Like everybody else I call these flowers Asters, and the true Aster I call Michaelmas Daisies.

But it is as well to know these things.

Annual Asters have been very popular flowers ever since they were first introduced. They were planted in enormous beds in the best French gardens and were also used as pot plants. Horace Walpole saw a 14 acre garden in France in which every walk was lined by pot-grown Asters. I don't know who counted them for him but he said there were nine thousand pots. Shades of gardeners content with humble wages!

Everybody loves a lover, they say: everybody certainly loved Asters. Pierre d'Incarville, French missionary and plant collector, Phillip Miller of the Chelsea Physic Garden, Dutchmen, Scots, Hanbury, Walpole, Frenchmen again. Where there were gardens and gardeners there were Asters. And, praise be, there still are!

The set-up has been, as it has with so many other flowers, complicated by the plant breeders who have developed so many lovely forms that you hardly know which to grow. I will adopt Culpeper's frequent dismissal, 'This is so well known, that time will be mispent in writing a Description of it.'

You look at the picture on the seed packet (or catalogue) you pays your money and you takes your choice.

And growing it is simple. If you want early flowers you sow

seed in a greenhouse or frame in March, prick off the plants into boxes and plant them out about late May. If you will be content with rather later flowers, then sow your seed direct in the beds outdoors as soon as the soil warms up—mid-May perhaps. This way, though few gardeners use it, I believe you get sturdier plants and stronger flowers. Only beware slugs as the seed germinates.

THE SHASTA DAISY

Chrysanthemum maximum is the full title of the Shasta Daisy. While it is widely grown it is such a good-tempered creature that it is not appreciated as it should be. I suppose we have been apt to regard it as just an ordinary Daisy on a large scale. So it is, but what a Daisy! And how handsome the plant is in high summer, and how tall and graceful the stems and how perfect in form and colour the flowers. And how excellent for cutting.

It is a job to appreciate what comes free, gratis and for nothing. When I came to my present garden there were a number of colonies of particular fine Shasta Daisies. I thought there were rather too many and began to thin their ranks. Some I gave away, some I threw away. There were less and less, and then suddenly one year I felt there was something missing from the border. It was more dull—ugly gaps where once it had been gay with flowers. The Shasta Daisies had gone. Very humbly I hunted out such bits and pieces as were left and began to build up my stock again. We are still not quite up to strength but things are improving.

These plants are excellent for lending interest to one of those awkward spots where more temperamental beauties are not at home. I have some growing at the edge of tree shade and they make a good show between a grassy bank and some Azaleas in the background. And once a friend asked for something for a ghastly clay bank where nothing would grow and I told him to dig it and add plenty of fertiliser and then I gave him a dozen of my Shasta Daisy plants and he put them in like Contrary Mary's pretty maids, all in a row. Now there is a hedge, two or three feet tall and covered with enormous flowers for at least two months every summer.

I'm boasting of course. Why not? I've had my failures, too: may as well make the most of the successes.

The tall Shasta Daisies need no staking—not in the positions in which I grow them. In wind-swept places I should think a bit of string tied round each clump would be enough—or the ubiquitous pea sticks.

The double Daisies, Esther Reed and Horace Reed, which I introduced in place of my undervalued singles are not so sturdy. There have been some sprawly clumps of those lying this way and that, and earth-soiled blooms after summer rains. For those I now use circles of narrow wire netting so that the plants grow inside a fence of the netting as it were. This netting is not tall, about a foot to eighteen inches, is not obtrusive and I usually leave it in place all the time.

The doubles are splendid flowers and most gardeners think much more highly of them than of the old-fashioned singles. But I am not sure. As I have said I started to throw the singles away and then wanted them back. There is something very fine in the very simplicity of their blooms, a purity of form that makes Esther Reed and her family a bit overblown sometimes.

Chrysanthemums are so closely associated with China and Japan that one thinks of the word Shasta as belonging to one of those countries, but it is not. It is a village, also I believe a county, in California where an American gardener named Burbank had a nursery. The flower had been introduced from the Pyrenees in 1816 and about the end of the century Burbank worked on it, hybridising with similar Japanese and American species until he got the Shasta Daisy we enjoy today. All credit to him but our own wild Ox-eye Daisy, which boasts the title *C. leucanthemum* is a very similar plant and flower, and is by no means at the tail end of the Daisy chain. In fact if your fancy is for something slightly less heavy than the Shastas a group of Ox-eyes, weed or not, will by no means disgrace your garden. I, who have grown it in mine, say so!

PYRETHRUM

The Pyrethrum is a very pretty Daisy flower, single or double, that is available in delicate shades of most colours except blue.

It is a favourite cut flower and is sold in enormous numbers at florists and off barrows every summer. A description should not be necessary, yet who grows them? I cannot think of one garden in my own district that boasts so much as a single group of this pretty and reputedly easy plant. I realise the people in the cut-flower trade must raise them in their hundreds of thousands, but perhaps they are a catch crop in greenhouses, for I have seen my share of nurseries and a field, say, or even a large bed of them would be as gay as a rainbow. But I never saw either.

No doubt the flower-growing districts of the south-west raise their share, but with their climate, saving the scourge of a sea-breeze or two, they should be able to grow anything.

I have an idea that this plant is not as easy as most Daisies are. I have put plants in often enough and for a season they do well, and the next year they may be there, but certainly not as vigorous, and after that, they do not appear, and you forget you had them till you see some flowers for sale on a stall. Now my soil is strong heavy stuff: in winter it is cold, often wet and it warms very slowly. It never dries out and it suits some things. But among the plants that are not happy in it are Pyrethrums. I think they need warm light soil containing a good proportion of humus (compost or rotted manure) and they should be given a spot where they will have as much sun as is going, and they should be right out of cold winds.

This plant is worth a little trouble. The flowers are so gay, and so good for cutting and with a little attention such as removing dead flowers promptly, blooms come out until autumn. A plant worth having.

It was introduced from the Caucasus region early in the nineteenth century, but, going by the pictures we have, was not a notable beauty. Its history is the history of so many popular flowers: it sort of hung on to existence in a few gardens for decades and then suddenly somebody woke to its possibilities. The Pyrethrum seems to have become popular about the 1870s or a little earlier and by then many named varieties were on the market. These seem to have thinned out (quite rightly, too many flowers are grown in too many varieties), but William Robinson named about fifty.

Nobody knows how long ago the Pyrethrum plant was grown for use as an insecticide, but it was an ingredient in a Persian insect-powder in very early times. The flower heads were cut just before they opened, dried and powdered. Now who found out that that would kill small insects? I have heard that in both world wars crops were grown in Kenya to make pyrethrum powder and it was of the utmost importance. Anyone who can remember soldier tales from the trenches in World War I, will realise how necessary a strong deterrent against fleas was necessary. The men really did suffer from the attentions of the little beasts and I believe de-lousing was a routine start to every man's spell out of the trenches. In the last war it was used a great deal to destroy flies that would have spread diseases such as typhus.

D.D.T. was a great discovery and nobody would deny the good work that was done with it, but it killed friends as well as foes. Also it can accumulate in the bodies of men and of animals and its use is not without danger. It may be on its way out. If I have to use poisons (I seldom do) I prefer pyrethrum and derris which are of vegetable origin and do not seem to affect the larger animals. They must, of course, kill off friends as well as foes, but small ones only. You do not hear of bees being annihilated by derris or pyrethrum as they were by D.D.T. All the same derris (made from the powdered flowers of the Derris plant) must be pretty deadly if used strong. In its native Malaya it was used as a fish poison. Placed in rivers it stupefied the fish. But it did not make them unfit for food. That sounds odd until you remember that many poisons—alcohol for instance—wouldn't!

Golden Rod, or Solidago is one of the easiest of the Compositae. It is not a choice plant—it is too free with its favours for that—but it is such a good-tempered, cheerful old thing, and is so colourful and it grows so readily anywhere that a corner might well be spared for a good-sized clump, though I would not say it should be encouraged everywhere, and self-sown seedlings must be weeded out promptly.

Long ago it was valued by the herbalists as a wound medicine and you can't read all they wrote about it without feeling there must have been some good quality in it. Turner described the healing drink that German physicians made from it. Gerard records that in Bucklersbury, the London herb-market, the dry herb was sold for half a crown an ounce, and he added that once they found it grown wild in England 'no man will give halfe a crowne for a hundred-weight of it, which plainly setteth forth our inconstancie and sudden mutabilitie, esteeming no longer of anything, how pretious soever it be, than whilest, it is strange and rare.'

Fair comment!

Culpeper says, 'It is a Sovereign wound-herb, inferior to none, both for inward and outward hurts, green Wounds, and old Sores, and Ulcers are quickly cured therewith.' He also wrote that 'Venus claims the Herb, and therefore to be sure, it restores Beauty lost.'

But how it can be made to do that he omits to mention.

Four notable annuals are members of the Daisy family though the position is a little complicated here because most species better known as perennials have also annual varieties. The four I am thinking about however are well known, widely grown, very ornamental and pretty, useful for beds and borders and all are easy to grow.

The Calendula is generally called the Scotch Marigold but I have never heard why. Some authorities have said that it was introduced from the Continent about 1570 but it was a familiar flower long before, and in most western countries at that. It was probably developed from a wild flower; quite a lot of wild yellow Daisies are very similar, and its early growers were concerned with the stomach rather than aesthetics. Swedish dockers in the fourteenth century used it because it 'draweth out of ye heed wikked hirores'—which I take to be horrors or humours. Sniffed well and deeply in the morning it kept you free from fevers during the day. It was an important ingredient in a medicine to keep the 'pestilence' away. The herbalist Turner mentions it as a hair dye to make the hair yellow by those 'not beyinge content with the natural colour, which God hath gyven them.' So evidently gentlemen preferred blondes then as now. The Dutch used the dried petals in 'broths, physical potions and for divers other potions'. Charles Lamb speaks of 'detestable marigolds in the pot,' and Cobbett thought little of the double form but recommended the single ones for cookery.

And so on . . . everybody knew Marigolds; everybody grew them; everybody ate them in one form or another. Barring the last (and perhaps we might do worse) we should do the same. Like Reginald Arkell's Gladys with her Sweet Peas we can just shove them in 'and golly how they grow.'

Tagetes are also called Marigolds but they are a different species. The African Marigold did not come from Africa and the French Marigold did not come from France. Both are from Mexico, so both presumably arrived together some time in the sixteenth century. I do not grow French Marigolds—they are not my style—but I love the fat blowsy Africans—in fact blowsy is not fair; they make handsome plants and have beautiful flowers. Their only drawback is in being yellow when so much else in the garden (except Sweet Peas!) is flaunting it in the same colour dress; much has been made of the unpleasant scent of Tagetes: 'Poisonous scent' says Parkinson; 'These flowers stink' (Hanbury); 'a naughtie strong and unpleasant savour' according to Lyte. Some ancient writers claimed that the smell indicated that the plants were poisonous, and Gerard has a yarn about a cat that died after eating some flowers mixed with cheese. A tall story. I like old Gerard: he was a good gardener and remains a good entertainer, but a few of his stories are so tall the summits are nearly out of sight—as with his account of barnacle geese which, said he, hatched out of wrecked ship timbers at the seaside —'that which I have seene with mine eies . . . I dare confidently avouch.'

As to the cultivation of Scotch and French Marigolds there is no difficulty at all except that they are half hardy annuals and must be started under glass.

The Helichrysum is one species of Everlasting Flowers. These also are best grown as half-hardy annuals. They are natives of the Mediterranean regions and were brought to this country as dried specimens long before anyone had seed to grow them. In ancient times the plants were of great importance because the dried flowers could be used when no others were available. They were used as garlands in worship of the gods so were reverenced more than they are today. They are easy to grow and they must be cut before the flowers are too advanced, also the colours tend to fade. But a posy of the stiff papery flowers is a cheerful sight on a cold winter day. If you *should* happen to like plastic flowers then good luck to you, have them, but you would find a bunch of everlastings much nicer.

Heleniums are very useful border flowers. They go on increasing from year to year but they do like feeding and I have an idea that they do better if they are dug up and divided occasionally because old colonies have a habit of dying out in some gardens. The flowers vary from the pure yellow of *H. pumilium magnificum* to the tawny red of Morheim Beauty, and in between there is a variety of two-coloured flowers with bands of orange and yellow. They come in late summer at a time when the border is losing a lot of its colour and a few groups, discreetly placed, can cheer things up a lot when earlier beauties are becoming subdued. They are splendid cut flowers.

The Rudbeckia is not dissimilar. This is the Cone Flower and is easy to distinguish from other Daisy types because of the cone of central florets. This is an even better cut flower than Helenium but unfortunately the best of the family—the flowers stay fresh in water literally for weeks—is a tall lanky plant that stands awkwardly head and shoulders above everything else. I have had plants 7 feet and more tall. The solution is obvious: grow a colony of them by themselves where their height will not matter. Other Rudbeckias are more modest in height, and *R. purpurea* has purple flowers instead of the more usual yellow. The very tall variety (6–8 feet), flowering in September, is called Autumn Sun. *R. deamii* is about half that, while Goldquille is double. They are all excellent border plants, but like Helenium, all have the tendency to die away once they are exhausted.

The plant originally came from Canada though no doubt it is found in other parts of America. Parkinson acquired plants from Tradescant who had his from the noted French gardener Vespasian Robin. Quite a journey! Some of the species were highly valued by the Red Indians as medicines: in fact they were to them very important herbs. One of the uses was for snake-bites, and according to a modern herbalist Mrs C. F. Leyel, it is a remedy for septicaemia. I do not know if this has ever been tested scientifically, but if not I think it would be worth a try.

Not that our modern drugs, often synthetic are not wonderful, but some of them *can* have nasty side-effects, while herbal remedies as a rule cure—or if you overdo it, kill outright!

A book about travels in America about 1819 says that boatmen on the Missouri used a medicine from Rudbeckia to counteract 'unpleasant consequences from their intercourse with the Squaws.'

That's not exactly crystal clear but one can make a fair guess at what the author meant.

You start on the Daisy family and suddenly realise that like Sinbad the Sailor you have the Old Man of the Sea on your shoulders. Not that I am worried; there are so many useful members that you could plant a garden of them and nothing else. But there are other flowers of other families I want to write about, so this Old Man I really must get rid of. The ornamental thistles, *Echinops ritro* with flowers like purple globes I will pass by, also the Cornflowers, but many-coloured Coreopsis must be included. There are both annual and perennial forms, and of course the latter are the most valuable because they *are* perennial, though in many soils they are not long-lived. They were introduced from America in the early seventeenth century and became very popular very quickly. The American name I'm told is Tickweed, and Coreopsis means bug-like and both labels refer to the shape of the seeds.

The Gaillardia is another N. American Daisy, not dissimilar to Coreopsis, Helenium and Rudbeckia. It is a useful border flower, gay, colourful and easy, often not long-lived but cheap to replace for it can be grown quickly from seed. There are both annual and perennial varieties.

Cosmos, or Cosmea, I think is Mexican. This is well-known everywhere. It is a half hardy annual and so far as I know there is no perennial form—not that are any use in gardens, anyhow. They are tall, graceful, excellent for cutting, have a long season in bloom, will grow almost anywhere . . . 'Come the full stop' as Salarino said when his friend was reciting Antonio's praise. But really, I can hardly think of a fault except that the wind will blow the plants down in a windy spot—and that could happen to any of us.

Erigerons do not need much description. They are rather like Michaelmas Daisies that have come out before their time; they flower in early summer. There used to be some very washy colours but lately these have been improved and there are a few good purples to be had. They are very useful mid-season flowers for the border and their height—about 18 inches—makes it easy to fit them in. Fleabane is the common name so they may have been used in the wars against those lively little creatures when they were more formidable pests than they are now.

Edelweiss (*Leontopodium*) was once for some reason regarded as a romantic and difficult Alpine plant and a few amateur collectors have risked their lives (and I believe some have lost them) collecting the plant in the Alps. Well it is not difficult and the best way to acquire it is not to climb a rock face on the Matterhorn but to sow a packet of seed. If Alpine associations were absolutely necessary you could gather the seed in a Swiss upland meadow. Why the plant was regarded as romantic I have never learned. Reginald Farrar introduced a scented form from Tibet for it is a Himalayan as well as an Alpine plant.

A Daisy flowered plant that I like very much but which most gardeners seem to think nothing of is Feverfew or Featherfew. Both names have been used. Gerard used the heading Featherfew and wrote of it as Feverfew and this is the name given to it in a modern book, R. D. Meikle's *Garden Flowers* in The Kew Series. I do not think there is much doubt that it was once a garden plant but it seeds itself so freely that it can become a weed —though it is easily got rid of. I cannot think of any garden, except my own, where I have seen it growing, and I collected mine from the garden of a deserted cottage a score or more years ago. It is a feathery leaved little plant about 18 inches high and my variety has leaves as yellow as golden privet. In summer each plant grows bushy and is completely covered with white-petalled Daisy flowers a little larger than a wild Daisy. The crushed leaves are very fragrant and there used to be a theory that rabbits objected strongly to it. True maybe, but when rabbits were a common pest they managed to stifle their objections in my garden.

It was once a notable herb and I believe, from the way Gerard

mentions 'divers vaine and trifling things' that some of its uses
have been forgotten. He recommended it for Vertigo also 'it is
good for such as be melancholike, sad, pensive and without
speech.' Culpeper also said it was good for vertigo and agreed
with Gerard that it was a remedy for 'Melancholly and heviness
or sadness of spirits.'

Last, but certainly not least, the head of the tribe, the common
Daisy. Our own wild species has been known and loved from
the earliest times and the Anglo-Saxon name for it was
Daezeseze. To gardeners it has been a weed: to poets an inspira-
tion. As long as men have cultivated grass and cut it and tried to
make lawns they have been trying to get rid of Daisies and it is a
humbling thought, or an encouraging one, according to how you
look at these things, to reflect that we seem to be no nearer success than when we started. What a pity, from the gardener's point
of view, that it grows so easily and flowers so freely. A meadow
full of Daisies . . . a Daisy-covered lawn (what's the difference!).
It is a sight to lift the heart but only children and poets have had
the perception to realise the fact. If it were difficult to grow and
slow to flower all the rest of us would love it, but then we are an
ungrateful crowd and what is given freely we do not want.

What a lot could be written about this very ordinary but very
beautiful little flower. It is apparently edible and has in the past
been used as a salad herb though not, I imagine, a very choice
one. The name *Bellis* (our wild Daisy is *Bellis perennis*) is from
the Latin word for war and that is because it was in early times
regarded as a wound herb. Gerard said that 'Daisies do mitigate
all kinde of paines, but especially in the joints, and gout, if they
be stamped with new butter unsalted, and applied upon the
pained place.' According to Culpeper 'The greater wild Daisie is
a Wound Herb of good respect, often used in those Drinks or
salves that are for Wounds, either inward or outward,' and later
he adds, 'An Oyntment made herof doth wonderfully help al
Wounds that have inflamations about them.'

I keep reading (and quoting) these recipes. I don't know why
I don't try a few of the simple ones sometimes. Perhaps I will!

I think Gerard's reference to 'The same given to little dogs
with milke, keepeth them from growing great,' is a bit of sym-

The Keukenhof at Tulip time

Mossy Saxifrage is excellent for banks or as ground cover

Sweet Rocket, an
old-fashioned
favourite
for early summer

Ornithogalum umbellatum, Star of Bethlehem: an easy and pretty bulbous plant

De Caen Anemones, the most colourful flowers of early summer

Allium moly, yellow, an easy and decorative member of the Onion family

Iceland Poppies: yellow poppies that will flower happily under shrubs

pathetic magic. He said the plant 'was called in old time Bruise-wort'. The reason, or presumed reason, is easy to work out.

There are of course garden Daisies, but I do not think they have the true beauty of the wild ones. The large-flowered varieties are pleasant enough things for edgings and so on but they are more novelties than flowers to be valued highly: they are flowers to delight children. A few small-type double Daisies have been developed and some of them are charming—in the right place. Dresden China with pink flowers was much enjoyed a few years ago. But I do not seem to have seen it lately. The difficulty is to know exactly where to grow them; they are little use in the border where they would be overlooked and the Alpine purists get so cross if we put them in the rock garden. For a window box gardeners want the fat giant ones. I had one once called Rob Roy, something like Dresden China but a deep red. The best thing to do if you enjoy these small varieties is to get a packet of seeds of the miniatures. From that all sorts of delightful little flowers should turn up.

Let Master Geoffrey Chaucer have the last word:

'Of alle the floures in the mede,
Than love I most these floures whyte and rede
Swiche as men callen daysies in our toun.'

It only remains to add that when you can put your foot on nine Daisies at the same time, spring has arrived.

Chapter 6: THE SWEET PEA

My father always grew a row of Sweet Peas in his garden and the way he did it was this. He dug a trench across the bed, often one of the vegetable beds and spread a thick layer of farmyard manure in it. He then raked (at least I think he did. I wasn't much interested in gardening!) a little soil over the manure. On this he sowed Sweet Pea seeds rather thickly. If I remember rightly he bought the seeds at the village post office for a few pence, though later an enterprising firm of seedsmen at St Albans—the name was Ryder; you may have heard it—introduced what they called P.P. seeds. The letters stood for Penny Packet and that was what they charged and my Dad who knew a good thing when he found it used Ryder's P.P. seeds for years. And he had some hard things to say when they raised the price to tuppence!

Well, that's by the way: having sown his seeds he raked some soil over them and patted it down. All this (I think) about March. In a few weeks the seedlings were coming up thick and fast and in a few weeks more we went to a local wood and cut a bundle of bushy hazel sticks. It must have been early because there were no leaves on the sticks and this was in a south Pembrokeshire valley that had a climate so balmy you could hardly throw down a banana skin without it taking root.

The pea sticks were stuck along the row of seedlings, two rows of sticks, one each side and the plants grew and twined their tendrils on the sticks and in a short time, about the beginning of June probably, the Sweet Peas were in flower and remained in flower until autumn. All that time they were an absolute rainbow of colour, and we cut enormous bunches by the score. And the scent was delicious.

Now I give all that information in full because you can still grow Sweet Peas in that way and still get the same, easy, colourful, fragrant results. Some people do grow them that way of course; you can see them in cottage gardens every summer. The flowers are not small; they do not have short stems, but I think most growers would agree that the scent is not quite what it was. Some gardeners say it is, but even such an expert as Charles Unwin admitted in a little book he wrote a few years ago* that the older varieties had more scent than the new ones. He was given some home-saved seeds in a Cambridgeshire village. They bore small flowers with poor colours but 'until then I had never appreciated to the full how sweet peas obtained their name'.

Mr Unwin also points out that years ago every cottager had his so-casually grown row of Sweet Peas—and that today every cottager has not.

In a way Sweet Peas can be compared with Chrysanthemums. You can do it the easy way and get very good results, or you can do it the hard way and get very good results.

When I started to grow Sweet Peas I did it, naturally, the way I had seen it done at home. The only difference I remember was that I had a lot of trouble saving my seedlings from slugs and I never remember my Daddy having that trouble—and he was not the sort of chap to bear troubles in stoical silence!

Now we come to the other extreme. I went to a flower show and the Sweet Peas on exhibition had stems about eighteen inches long and the thickness as with Goliath's spear, was like a weaver's beam. The flowers were so large you could have become airborne had they been fastened to your shoulders, the colours were dazzling, and though the scent was not as strong as it should have been, I was so overcome with the magnificence of these lovely blooms that nothing would do but I must grow some myself.

In time I learned how to grow them. Some gardeners have little secrets; some pretend to have little secrets, though frankly the most of it is common sense. Some gardeners will tell you all they know and help you all they can. A few won't but I am not sure they *are* real gardeners.

* *Sweet Peas.* Chas. W. J. Unwin, Amateur Gardening Handbooks No. 36.

There are a number of slight variations in the methods of growing first class exhibition Sweet Peas, but I learned a bit from this one and a bit from that and this was eventually how I went about it.

I bought my seeds early in autumn, I bought them from an expert grower, and I bought the best I could get.

In October I sowed my seeds, as many as I wanted plants, one seed in a two or three inch pot. I did not soak them nor chip them and I found that germination was pretty nearly a hundred per cent. They were started in a greenhouse but when they were growing strongly I moved them to the coolest spot I could find, and often this was a cold frame. When really bitter frosts were about I would cover the frame with a few sacks. Where the little seedlings were growing strongly I pinched out the tips. This caused them to branch, and so most plants had two or three stems.

In November I prepared the trench (or trenches if I wanted one or two rows). That took me at least a week of my spare time, sometimes longer.

I took out a trench three feet wide, I put the soil on one side. I then dug the trench another spade deep putting that soil on the other side. I then dug another spade (or fork) depth breaking it up thoroughly but did not take it out of the trench. I scattered lime in the bottom of the trench and a little on the soil that had been dug out on either side. I put a lot of good farm manure in the bottom of the trench and mixed it in well. I sprinkled bone meal on the other soil and then put it back loosely in the same order it had come out. My Sweet Pea trench to be, was by this time looking a right old mess, and of course was like a ridge of rough soil. In time it sank nearly level and by the time the frosts had had a go at it it was in superb condition, and by March I could rake it level.

The plants were set out at the beginning of April in a double row in what had been the middle of the trench, that is, they had about a foot of cultivated soil on each side. The plants had made short sturdy growth over the winter so needed some small bushy twigs for support. For each plant a tall seven or eight foot cane (I used hazel sticks: they cost nothing) was given as a support and as the plants grew they were tied to the canes. Later I used a tall length of wire netting and wire rings to fasten in the stems. As the plants grew all the side shoots in the leaf axils were rubbed out leaving one flower stem to a leaf axil. All tendrils were cut off the leaf tips, support always being given by tying or by wire rings. I did not feed because I had been really generous with manure and I do not think I ever had to water (you don't need to when you cultivate the soil deeply.)

A rather tiresome job was that when the plants grew too tall for the canes they had to be untied, and lowered and tied to canes further along the row so that they could still have support.

I was never disappointed in my results. The flowers were as good as you could find anywhere and were something with which I could show off—modestly, 'oh-they-aren't-nearly-as-good-as-last-year's' sort of thing. I never entered any in a show. For show work you need an enormous quantity of plants.

I may say that I have not grown them in this way for many years. It is lovely when you have lots of energy and time but it is hard work and I can get good flowers (*not* exhibition blooms) for much less trouble. Generally I grow a couple of dozen plants in small pots in early spring and these I plant out in one or two circular groups in the borders in April. I put pea sticks round them and leave them alone and they do very well giving colourful groups to the garden and lots of flowers for the house. You have heard of children who were born with silver spoons in their mouths: well, my wife was born with a pair of flower-cutting scissors on finger and thumb, and even she does not grumble about not having enough Sweet Peas.

Between those two methods there are a number of other ways you can grow them, and no doubt there is room for experiment. I believe some of the new dwarf varieties will grow quite well in containers such as vases and large tubs but they need good soil and plenty of water and a little feeding. There is a really dwarf type generally called Little Sweetheart, or something like that, which grows some 8–12 inches tall but even better is the one called Knee-hi, which name is as pointless as the spelling because if grown well they are a lot nearer waist high. The seed merchants say they do not need sticks but my experience is that they are a lot better if they have some support. These miniature plants have flowers quite as large as those on the taller plants, and bear as many as nine blooms on a stem.

You can grow Sweet Peas as trailers in a largish bed, not supporting them at all but allowing them to wander where they will on the face of the earth. This can be a wonderfully colourful way of growing the plants—the flower stems of course grow upwards —but when not successful they can look rather messy. Also they are seldom close enough to smother weeds so those are apt to raise their ugly heads.

Quite by chance I discovered for myself that Sweet Peas are lovely in a greenhouse. I had bought a house with a large empty conservatory-type greenhouse and had paid so much for the house that I had hardly enough money left for a packet of Cabbage seed let alone fill a big greenhouse with suitable plants. I put a row of autumn sown Sweet Pea plants in a bed next to a wall and added a length of wire netting for them to cling to if they should grow. They flourished exceedingly. In fact the flowers were about as good as any I have ever had because they were completely protected from any weather blemishes. Also they came out very early in summer.

You would think that from then on I would always have grown some in the greenhouse but I am afraid I do not. In the established garden, annuals, even the best, always suffer from the competition from more permanant subjects and the bed in which I grew those lovely Sweet Peas now contains a Vine *and* a Peach *and* a little tank with a Water Lily in it *and* some flourishing Arums that flower so well I can't bear to put them elsewhere. So you see as the Old Woman of the Shoe used to say: the place is a bit crowded.

We always quote the introduction of a plant as if it had had no existence before it reached our shores, but Sweet Peas were being gathered by children in the lanes outside Pompeii on the day that Vesuvius blew up and buried the city. And of course for thousands of years before that. The plant was a very ordinary wild flower of Sicily and probably of most parts of southern Italy. But it was a Sicilian priest and botanist, Father Cupani, who first noticed that it was rather a pleasant little thing and in 1699 sent some seeds to an Enfield schoolmaster, Dr Robert Uvedale. That early plant, it is said, was nothing notable as a floral beauty, but it did have that marvellous scent. By 1730 the flower had attracted a little notice and seeds were for sale. It does not appear to have won a lot of attention and it certainly was not a popular flower for more than a century after that. You cannot help wondering why a few gardeners continued to grow it, but probably its fragrance caused a few discerning people to go on.

The first man who really concentrated on improving this undistinguished member of the pea family was Henry Eckford. He seems to have started work about 1870, hybridising, selecting and so on, and others joined in the work so that at a great Sweet Pea Exhibition held in the Crystal Palace in 1900 there were 264 varieties on show. My word, when those Victorian gardeners got going they really went to town. There must be many scores of excellent varieties available today but I doubt if there are anything like 264. Of that number Eckford had raised 115.

In 1901 Silas Cole, gardener of Earl Spencer showed the waved flower he called Lady Spencer, and from that time the Spencer Sweet Peas with frilled petals took the place of those with smooth petals. Some discriminating gardeners did not care for the way things were shaping: the expert Charles Curtis in his famous book on Sweet Peas thought that beauty could develop into vulgarity. I believe his book came out before the first World War. What he would think of some of our modern varieties it is difficult to say, but on the whole I don't think we have much to grumble about. It is difficult to think of any flower that will give as great a reward for so little effort.

It is worth knowing that at least one of our most famous growers can still offer seed of the old fashioned super-scented kind, and can sell you the original kind sent here in 1699. So there is no excuse for any of us grumbling that Sweet Peas are not what they were.

Lathyrus latifolius is the Perennial Sweet Pea—only it is not sweet and though it is a useful little herbaceous climber it is completely shadowed by its annual relation and that is the only case I can think of where the annual variety of a flower eclipses the perennial species. Its colour anyhow is that magenta shade that is difficult to harmonise with anything else.

There is a perennial white form with dazzling white flowers and this is a very choice plant and worthy of a place in any garden.

The roots of some of the perennial peas are said to be edible but when we were children we were warned that Sweet Pea seeds were poisonous. Apart from the herbalists (and not all of them were reliable) country people never did know a lot about wild flowers and I think they told us most things were poisonous—just to be on the safe side! Peas and beans, of course, are first rate foods but in excess even they can upset delicate stomachs.

The roots of one of the vetches, *L. montanus,* were once chewed by Highlanders and this was said to keep hunger at bay for a long time. Possibly it has some narcotic quality but I have never known anyone who chewed it and have no urge to experiment for myself.

Chapter 7: THE DAFFODIL

To most of us the Daffodil is the sign that spring has really arrived, though in our climate it is a sign that often has to be taken down once or twice before it can be relied on. We buy the bulbs in autumn, off the multiple-store counters if we are casual, from a specialist bulb merchant if we are a little more fussy or want the lesser-known varieties. We plant them in the garden a few inches deep during the autumn and by about Easter—Daffodils in flower in the garden. It is as simple as that.

Further, if they have been planted in moderately fertile soil they will flower the next year, and the next . . . and the next . . . and so *ad infinitum.* Each year the clump that has developed from the original bulb gets larger and larger. Sometimes they begin to produce more leaves than blossoms and then is the time to dig up the whole lot (*after* the leaves have died down) split up the bulbs, replant them and start all over again. How long a colony will go on flowering is anybody's guess but I know that when I was a boy in Pembrokeshire we used to pick the double flowers in fields in spots where cottages had once stood, though they might have tumbled down half a century before, leaving little more than grassy mounds to show where once there had been a home. Those old Daffodils were nearly always double flowers, deep yellow, as lush as Cabbages and very strongly scented. There was by the way a tradition in some places that this scent was, if not actually poisonous, very bad for you. It was not a superstition in our village—though my word, we had some beauties of our own!—and most people enjoyed the perfume. The deep yellow flowers themselves were not highly valued: I suppose they were common. What were considered choice were single trumpet Daffodils but they were only found in gardens and not in all gardens at that. We had not reached the stage where you could buy a few bulbs cheaply in any shop and we certainly had not reached the stage where farm labourers ordered them through catalogues, and, personally, though my father did have catalogues sent to him—he was after all the village schoolmaster, and by common consent a man of great learning!—I never saw one in which Daffodils were listed.

The double Daffodils we gathered on the old cottage sites were, I thought, when I came to know a little more of the subject, the ones praised by or raised by one of the Tradescants, the king's gardeners in the seventeenth century, but it could equally well have been Van Sion raised by a man called Vincent Sion about 1620.

We had another local Daffodil in Pembrokeshire and that I understand was a true species and not a garden variety. It was the Tenby Daffodil and I believe is still occasionally listed as *Narcissus obvallaris*. Half a century ago when there was practically no cut flower trade in out of the way places men used to dig up the Tenby Daffodil bulbs by the sackful and send them away. In time the plant became rare and today you would be lucky to find any growing wild. The Tenby Daffodil probably suffered more because it is a very choice flower very much like a King Alfred in colour and shape, but much smaller.

Herefordshire still has its wild Daffodils growing in thousands in fields and woods but these though a marvellous sight when all are in flower together, are not really choice blooms by themselves and so, though some women pick them to sell by the bunch the bulbs are seldom dug up.

Growing Daffodils in the average garden is not so much 'how' as 'where'. The whole point is that to keep the bulbs healthy the plant must be allowed to die down naturally after flowering. Sometimes, and in some places and seasons, the leaves take a very long time to die.

Where there is room, say in an orchard or a paddock, an ideal method is naturalising. That is to say scatter the bulbs, here and there; up and down, and then you plant them. Where it will be necessary to cut the grass fairly early in summer it is best to plant groups. At least you can go round groups with your mower or scythe and avoid the tufts of leaves.

If the grass is grazed by animals, a pony or a few sheep for example, I do not know that Daffodils are suitable for planting. The leaves contain crystals of calcium oxalate, which are harmful, perhaps actually dangerous. I doubt if animals would graze the leaves themselves because they are bitter—so I am told—but they could get the odd mouthful of dying foliage. This business of poisons in plants is a little difficult to sort out. Poisonous the Daffodil sap may be but slugs will eat the stems and the flowers and to the best of my knowledge our slug population is not falling.

I have tried planting Daffodils in grass on a bank at the end of my main lawn and though they made a brave show in spring there was the old trouble of untidy dying leaves.

I have now settled in my garden for two sites. One is a long bank planted with a few trees and some very hearty Rhododendrons. I think the bulbs must suffer a little from competition from the roots of the shrubs but I generally put some fertiliser over them after they have flowered. Occasionally we have to cut out some Rhododendron branches that are hiding Daffodils and sometimes we cut one of them right back to ground level and leave it to make a fresh start—which it does without delay and with great vigour.

All my other Daffodils I plant in the border. They started out as small groups and most are now large ones. Some were only single bulbs when they were put in, for I often treat myself to a solitary bulb of a fairly new variety, cheap really at four or five shillings, and these soon increase. They grow between the established border plants and they flower in early spring before their herbaceous companions are more than a few inches high. When the leafy plants are growing strongly the Daffodils are over and their dying leaves—always their most unsightly feature—are hidden. If they are not hidden they can usually be tucked out of sight. So I get a colourful border from very early in the year and of course the bulbs get a lot of benefit from the compost and fertiliser that is given to the other plants.

If you do have a few choice bulbs you have no place for, it is well worth having a good look to see if there is a spot near, or opposite to, a window for them. They can be a great pleasure in bad spring weather. I bought a dozen of the less usual varieties at the Spring Royal Horticultural Society Show at Vincent Square once, and dug out a bit of rough shrubbery opposite a window and planted them there. It is almost as good as having them in the house.

Daffodils have this in common with Roses that it has now become almost impossible to work out the ancestry of anything. I don't know that it is a matter of great concern. If you would become a specialist you should buy a classic on the subject and study it. Such a volume is *Daffodils and Narcissi* by M. J. Jefferson-Brown. He published his book in 1953 and it has recently been brought up to date. I should think it contains about everything. As far as I can find out the first literature devoted entirely to the flower was written by the botanist William Turner in 1548. It was called *A Few Narcissi of Diverse Sortes* (I have never seen it) and I am told the number he knew was 24. Parkinson, nearly a century later, was able to describe about ninety. The Royal Horticultural Society now lists about 10,000 different varieties. I should think that eclipses the Roses. But who wants (or grows) them all? I cannot help feeling that with kinds so prolific an effort should be made to get rid of some of the duplicates and some of the dross. But I would not like to be the chap with the job of deciding what must go overboard!

I go to my favourite bulb catalogue when I want a few new or extra special flowers. As far as I am concerned I simplify my flowers into long trumpets, medium trumpets, and those with tiny flat trumpets like the little scented Poets Narcissi. There are singles and doubles in all of these. Also there are the miniature tiny species, suitable for grassy banks or the rock garden. Whoever draws up my catalogue is fairly reasonable and he keeps things *moderately* simple, but even he sub-divides each class rather more than *I* need. Trumpet Daffodils, for example, are Division 1. Division 1A are those with yellow trumpets; Division 1B are the flowers with a white perianth and a colourful corona, 1C has a white perianth and a white corona . . . and so on. I lent my catalogue to a fairly uncomplicated chap but he brought it back: 'I be getting in a right muddle,' he said. 'Better I stick to a few Shirley poppies.' He did not, of course, but you can see how he felt.

The best way to buy Narcissi of any sort is to go to a spring flower show and choose the ones you like from the trade exhibits.

The history of the Narcissus family can be traced back for as long as men have written about flowers. The Egyptians left it in their tombs; Homer praised it; Ovid told the story of the beautiful youth who fell in love with his own reflection and fell into the water and was drowned, and there are other ancient legends about it. Pliny seems to have been the first to mention the narcotic scent and said that was how the name originated.

The English name apparently derived from Asphodel and was originally 'Affodyl' and this seems to have caught on because we find 'Daffadowndylles' used quite early. It was a name that persisted and I have known old people use it and perhaps a few still do. It's a bit stretched out, but I prefer it to 'Daffs'. There is some doubt as to whether our wild Daffodils are true natives or whether the Romans introduced them. Most species seem to have originated in the Mediterranean region, but others have come from various parts of Asia.

The herbalists do not appear to have found much use for the plant though Gerard thought they helped to heal wounds and said the roots mixed with honey were good for burns, especially sunburn. But I have heard that people who have to pick large quantities get a skin irritation from the slimy sap so perhaps we had better love the flower for itself alone.

Chapter 8: THE TULIP

As with many other popular flowers so with the Tulips. There are too many kinds to choose from. For the specialist or for the gardener who has unlimited room and unlimited money to spend on them, this may be very fine, but if you only want a dozen or a hundred you feel like a boy with sixpence in a big sweetshop: you don't know what to have.

This is not really a serious complaint. I am very glad that there are so many lovely flowers, so much colour, and sometimes scent, but occasionally the various types of Tulips are so similar that differences are of interest only to the botanist.

I suppose I see most of the bulb catalogues that are issued each year. They may be had for the asking and the gardener who does not know where to ask has only to look through any gardening magazine at the appropriate season to find offers of them coming from left, right and centre. A lot of them are illustrated, and most of them are interesting and some are really superb, with coloured illustrations of a very high quality. Once upon a time I was simple enough to wonder how these chaps could *possibly* afford to give away such lovely books but of course they don't. The cost of book production being what it is it would be impossible. We pay for them, you and I. That is, the cost must go on to the cost of the merchandise. Nobody said so but it must. And I for one don't grudge a penny of it.

Now I am (let us suppose) going to plant a few hundred Tulips to flower next spring so I go to my favourite catalogue to find what there is to offer.

I find a choice of,
   Early Single Tulips
   Early Double Tulips

Mid-Season Tulips
Darwin Tulips
New Darwin Hybrid Tulips
Lily-Flowered Tulips
Cottage Tulips
Multiflowered Tulips
Fringed Tulips
Broken-Coloured Tulips
Parrot Tulips
Late Double Tulips
Fosteriana Tulips
Kaufmanniana Tulips
Greigii Tulips
Viridifolia Tulips

And to round off, the wild Tulips or species listed under Botanical Tulip Species.

It is a fair old list, and I will not blame you if you wander off to the multiple stores, look at the pictures opposite the various trays and buy say a few dozen early doubles, and a few dozen Darwins.

The worst of it is that the bulb merchant is losing the rewards for his book and enterprise while *we* are missing some beautiful flowers.

I do not propose in these pages to offer a description of all the kinds I have just mentioned. If this were a book on Tulips or for Tulip enthusiasts only, I might do so but it is not.

So which of these flowers shall I recommend?

Well, undoubtedly the most useful types still for bedding, are the Darwins. They have been grown in our gardens since 1886. They are named in honour of Charles Darwin. They are so familiar as to need no description.

For early flowers, obviously it is best to plant a few labelled Early Flowering though if space is limited I do not think that they appear so much earlier than the Darwins to be worth bothering with. They are (for me) the ones to plant in pots and bowls for flowering in the greenhouse or in the house; singles and doubles being equally valuable and choice being a matter of taste. Both are nicely scented; I think the doubles perhaps last a little longer than the singles, though if they are in a cool room not long enough to matter.

Lily-flowered Tulips have pointed petals, some more so than others, and are perhaps a little more graceful than the Darwins but in colours there is no marked difference.

If you want something really different from the type, something unusual and eye-catching plant a bed of Parrot Tulips. These appeared first about 1665, and I believe they were developed from 'sports', that is, variations from the more familiar types. The flowers are fringed or scalloped in an almost indescribable way. I was about to write that they look like a Darwin whose petals have been chipped and chopped by a child with a pair of scissors but really they are not at all like that. In spite of the ripped edges the appearance is, if I may put it so, right—just as a Ragged Robin in the hedge looks right. Nature meant it to be so.

In spite of their respectable age of three hundred years comparatively few people grow them. A small bed is worth while in any garden. In full sunshine the mature blooms open out nearly flat, say as flat as a saucer and almost as wide. It is a breath-taking sight.

Fosteriana Tulips are a species that came from somewhere in Bokhara. They have been hybridised so are available in many colours now, but for real barbaric splendour I do not think there are many flowers to touch the original scarlet types. There is not a very wide choice but the best is a variety sometimes listed as Red Emperor and sometimes as Madame Lefeber.

The catalogue sums up the colour as 'magnificent and vivid blazing orange vermilion-scarlet, base black, bordered yellow.' One gets wary of superlatives but with that one I agree.

Kaufmanniana Tulips are, or started off as, species (or wild types). They are sometimes called Water-Lily Tulips. I think they are best for pockets in the rock garden, though unfortunately slugs love to eat the bulbs; they are also good for pot culture though not perhaps for forcing.

Viridifolia Tulips started as a species but hybridising has introduced a mixture of shades. They all have green or partly green petals and are most attractive in appearance. They generally attract a lot of attention at shows, and a bed of them would, I am sure, get a lot of notice in the garden.

So we are left with the true wild Tulips, generally listed as Botanical Tulips. How many there are in nature I do not know, though Patrick Synge's *Bulbs* lists about forty. But from a specialist bulb merchant you may have a choice from a score. Many of these should be grown in pockets in the rock garden, but nearly all will do well in pots in a cool greenhouse or an Alpine house. If you can possibly get to a good show like the Royal Horticultural Society holds each spring at Vincent Square you will be able to see most of them in flower. Catalogue descriptions are useful but not as good as seeing the blooms themselves. One of my own favourites is *Tulipa clusiana,* a Persian type, which the diplomat-gardener Clusius was growing in his garden in 1607. It is a lovely little thing with long pointed flowers of rather mixed colouring, reddish outside, white inside, and a group makes a very pleasant sight in late April. My other favourite is a Turkish species called *T. praestans.* This is unusual in that a number of flowers grow on one stem. The best to plant is the variety known as Fusilier which in colour is almost as fiery as *T. fosteriana.* It is however much smaller than fosteriana and is best for the rock garden or cool house culture.

There are no difficulties at all about growing Tulips. The bulbs are planted in good soil and they flower. Yet their culture is quite different from the culture of the Daffodil.

The first point to note is that they are not as suitable for naturalising. Their stately stiffness (they seldom sway in the wind as the Narcissi do) seems suited to formal beds. This instruction need not be taken too seriously. In my mixed border I have a few informal clumps that have grown and flowered happily for many years. But also I have planted groups that have died out. It is important if they are put among herbaceous plants to have them well to the front, for when they are in flower many plants are growing strongly and will hide anything behind them.

Experts say that they are the better for late planting, October, November or even December, so that early foliage is not damaged by frosts. Maybe so, but I have a few that come up in the same place year after year and I have never known one to be frost-damaged though in my district we get severe frosts, especially in early spring.

As a rule Tulips are not as long-lived as Daffodils but again I have to qualify the statement. In my last garden I had Tulips that came up year after year for a dozen years and more and apart from the fact that the flowers were smaller they lost none of their vigour. My present garden is colder and the soil is heavier and many rows of Tulips have died out.

Slugs eat Tulip bulbs and I am sure many of mine have gone to feed those gentry. The bulbs are natives of hot countries ranging from the Mediterranean across Asia as far as China. Many of these countries often have cold hard winters but they also have hot dry summers and the bulbs get a thorough baking. Whatever nice things Charles II said about our climate, sunbaking is something we seldom get—or not for long. All the time an exception, like sex, rears its ugly head. The Dutch do pretty well with the bulbs and they get some quite cool wet summers at times. So where are we?

Well we all have our little secrets and our little ways and in Tulip culture, for those who would like to plant the bulbs as permanent subjects, here is mine.

In their native countries I have been told recently the bulbs grow at least a foot deep. Many years ago a gardener told me the best way to plant Tulips was to dig out an area three feet deep. At this point memory fails me: either he said put in manure two feet deep, plant the bulbs, cover with a foot of soil . . . or he said put in manure a foot deep, plant the bulbs, cover with two feet of soil. Let's compromise: settle for a two foot deep bed, put in a foot of manure, plant the bulbs, cover with a foot of soil.

The point really is that being very ignorant in gardening matters, very credulous of what my betters told me and moderately energetic I did as I was told and those Tulips came up year after year, thicker and thicker until every bulb planted grew into an enormous clump. The individual flowers, though just as colourful, were smaller as time went on but those that were cut and put in vases grew in the water and were just as big as from new bulbs.

In my experience the method does work, and though it is hard labour it has to be done only once. But gardeners who suffer from lumbago should avoid it.

If you do try it have some bedding plants to put in when the Tulip leaves are dying: something easy like Marigolds (Calendulas) or Nasturtiums.

The history of the Tulip as a garden flower goes back some four hundred years when the Austrian diplomat, de Busbecq saw them in Turkish gardens, though it is almost certain that they were grown in eastern gardens long before that time. De Busbecq brought seeds and perhaps bulbs to Vienna, and Conrad von Gesner, whose name lives on in *Tulipa gesneriana* published a description of them. The man to whom we seem to owe the general introduction was the botanist Clusius, also commemorated by a species *T. clusiana*. He became Professor of Botany at Leyden and there is a story that he had a good stock of bulbs but wanted so much money for them that nobody could afford to buy them. The solution was simple: somebody stole some and so the Tulip, as a western flower, was launched. The early stocks came mainly from seeds.

The best-known story about the flowers is the Tulip Boom. Briefly this was the craze that took possession of the Dutch. They made the bulbs the object of speculation and prices reached such ridiculous figures that laws had to be made limiting the maximum price. It was £400 which if my guess at rate of exchange is correct was 4,000 florins. The madness lasted from about 1630 to 1637 and then ended abruptly and with the drop in prices many hundreds of the speculators were ruined. About a century later there was a revival of the craze but it never got quite as much out of hand as in the seventeenth century.

After that the sober Dutchmen (are they really as sober as all that?) got things under control and began the industry that was to make the Dutch the most important bulb growers in the world.

It is many, many years since I read Dumas' novel *The Black Tulip* but that has some interesting sidelights on the early Dutch bulb industry.

Some amusing (I'm not sure that is the right word!) stories have come down to us from the Tulip Boom days. There were tales of cooks who cooked bulbs worth a fortune but it does not speak very highly of Dutch cooks if they could confuse a Tulip with an Onion. Another gives an account of a sailor waiting in a Dutch merchant's office who picked up and ate a bulb lying on the desk thinking it was some sort of Onion, and of course it was a Tulip that had cost the merchant 4,000 florins. I hate to spoil a good story but a merchant who left 4,000 florins' worth of Tulip unguarded on an outer office desk deserved to lose it. On the other hand such events as their being cooked by mistake and eaten by mistake must have happened occasionally. I have never tasted a Tulip bulb myself but they are edible and I believe were used as food in Holland during the last war. The seventeenth century gardener Parkinson preserved some in sugar and found them very pleasant, 'fit to be presented to the curious'.

The bulbs were by no means cheap when the Tulip Boom came to an end. Hogg of Paddington writing about 1820 said that a collection could cost a thousand pounds. Since the bulbs increase quite rapidly from offsets and all are said to grow easily from seeds it appears that somebody was making a good thing out of it. Even as late as 1854 the catalogue of a Clapham nursery-man listed a few varieties at a hundred guineas each. But such a delightful state of affairs (for the growers!) could not last with such an easy plant and in the end prices dropped to a level that the ordinary gardener could afford.

Ah well, it was nice while it lasted, and it is even nicer for the majority of us that it did not last longer.

There does not appear to be any mention of the flower in ancient literature though perhaps if it was a common wild flower without any medicinal property there is no reason why it should be. I have heard that Solomon's Rose of Sharon was a Tulip, though for what reason I cannot imagine. People are always claiming that plants mentioned in the Bible were something else; I mentioned this earlier. The Lily of the Field was an Anemone; the Apple was an Apricot; the Rose was not a Rose. But why? Lilies, Apples and Roses as well as lots of common English garden flowers and fruits grow all over the near (and far) east.

I think some people like to be contradictory!

Chapter 9: HYACINTH, CROCUS AND SNOWDROP

In theory these three are as popular as Daffodils and Tulips but in practice they are bought in smaller numbers and planted less widely. With the Hyacinth I think the reason is twofold. The bulb is a lot dearer than most and in the open garden the bloom is often rather poor after its first season. With the other two it is probably because they are not as conspicuous (either bulbs or flowers) and tend to be overlooked.

Hyacinths are splendid flowers for formal beds. Their colours are vivid and gay and they have that incredibly rich scent. But to fill an open bed with even the cheapest bulbs would cost quite a nice little sum and I think the gardener, counting his pence, would buy a few for a bowl and settle for Tulips—which would probably cost him a quarter as much.

I am sure that the majority of Hyacinth bulbs go into pots and bowls, and very suitable they are for that kind of culture. Also you can get good value for money. One Hyacinth in a small pot will give a spike that will not be easily overlooked. Three is a notable sight and anything over half a dozen is practically an indoor garden. Not long ago I speculated on a cheap collection— actually I pushed out the boat and got *two* collections—that was being offered by a woman's magazine. They took an awful time a-coming and when they came they were small. My expectations did not run high. I put the lot in peat in a tub I happened to have handy. When spring came they made such a show of such enormous spikes that nobody would believe I had not wasted my substance on the very dearest top-size bulbs.

While on this subject a word on bulbs in containers may not

come amiss. Most gardeners know the simple technique but a few do not. The majority of spring bulbs will grow in containers and most will flower well indoors. And though there may be failures here and there, they are easy.

My own simple method may be helpful to those who have not tried indoor bulbs before.

1. Any container may be used, from an old Spode teapot to a tub or window box. If it has no drainage holes then you must be careful not to overwater.

2. Fill your container with light garden soil, compost, soilless compost, peat or bulb fibre. The compost, whatever it is should be damp, *not* wet, *not* dry.

3. Push your bulbs into the fibre so that their noses are just below soil level.

4. Put your container in any dark cool place and leave it for two or three months.

5. Bring it out of retirement and still keep it in a coolish place.

6. As the stems grow give warmer conditions.

Regarding Number 6 the art of having very fine flowers is not to try to force them too soon. As they grow you may give more heat, but it should never be a high temperature such as over a radiator and it should never be a dry heat. The professional gardener may force bulbs into flower early but he has the right conditions for forcing and the knowledge and experience necessary.

Generally I try to have a pot or two of Hyacinths each year. When the leaves have died down I plant the bulbs in some out-of-the-way corner and they flower—much less lushly than they did indoors—for many years. Sometimes they do not but after the old-soldier manner, simply fade away. There was, by the way, a Hyacinth Mania in Holland similar to the Tulip Mania but history never repeats itself exactly and prices never rose as madly.

There are, of course a few Hyacinth species, about 30 in all, but they are not common in gardens (I expect there are a few at Wisley and Kew) and are very rarely found listed in catalogues. There is a miniature variety known as the Roman Hyacinth, and others sometimes called Cynthella Hyacinths but I believe these are the same, or very closely related. They have much smaller flowers than the Dutch bulbs, and are the easiest to flower indoors. If the bulbs are planted early they can be coaxed into flower by Christmas.

Our native Bluebell is a Hyacinth or at least a close relative but the botanists have pushed the poor thing about and though the catalogues offer it under Scilla the above-named gentry have given it the label Endymion. Not that it matters: a Rose by any other name would smell as sweet and whatever they call it, it will remain the same lovely meadow flower that for some odd reason once had an almost pathological fascination for cyclists so that on late May evenings you used to see them pedalling home, hell-for-leather, with bunches as big as trusses of hay tied to their handlebars. I think the fashion, or habit or whatever it was has died out. Or perhaps the cyclists now all have cars and the Bluebells are still there but on the back seat. There used to be quite a hullabaloo about this annual despoiling of the Bluebell woods; it was good for quite a few indignant letters in the Press; but I do not think there ever was much danger. Bluebells increase so rapidly from offsets that it would take more than a few cyclists to wipe out the species.

The English Bluebell is not a flower for gardens. If you have a little wood or a wild bank or an odd corner where you would like a few easy flowers then they will make a pretty sight, but for borders there are more substantial inhabitants to be found. There is however a variety known as the Spanish Hyacinth, *Endymion hispanicus,* if you are fussy about correct names, and this is a larger flower, a larger plant in all respects and a few groups to the front of a border or under some shrubs will cheer things up a lot when the Daffodils have faded and the Lupins and Delphiniums have not come out. There are varieties in blue, in pink and in white. If you put them among the shrubs they will with luck seed themselves and increase.

By the way do not hunt round for Scotch Bluebells as mentioned in the Victorian music hall ballad and expect to see a Hyacinth. *That* is a Campanula . . . we couldn't manage without the botanists but they do make it hard for us, don't they?

'You have the Pyrrhic dance as yet;
Where is the Pyrrhic phalanx gone?'

So wrote Byron, who admired the warlike spirit and achievements of the ancient Greeks. I think I prefer their art and mythology. All the same I cannot quite see how the slightly erotic story of the Moon goddess who used to come down and kiss the youth Endymion and sleep by his side links up with our Bluebells. Hyacinth was a lovely youth loved by Apollo and Zephyr. He preferred Apollo so Zephyr deflected Apollo's quoit and the youth was slain. His blood became the flower.

Gerard said that the juice from Bluebell bulbs would 'serve to set feathers upon arrows instead of glew, and to paste bookes with.' He also repeated Dioscorides' opinion that the roots 'being beaten and applied with white wine, hinder or keep back the growth of haires.'

Most of us want to know how to *make* them grow!

THE CROCUS

On the whole the Crocus family is not too be-devilled by division. We have a choice of what are called the Dutch Crocus, which are the fat ones most of us grow; and a fair number of species. In the wild there are many of these. Some are rare and some are of interest only to botanists. Those we can buy easily for our gardens come down to about a score, though some have been hybridised and there is plenty of choice. *Crocus chrysanthus,* for instance, in the first catalogue I open may be bought in eleven varieties, but I doubt whether most gardeners would care much whether they were growing Blue Bird, or Blue Giant, or Blue Pearl.

In the garden they are flowers to naturalise. I do not think they are for lawns; the leaves can persist a long, long time and I am sure, from my personal experience, that the corms deteriorate if the leaves are not allowed to die completely. I used to think that a fairly good soil was needed but again I am not sure. My best colony of Dutch Crocuses grows in a bank facing east. The soil is dry and harsh and is filled with trees and shrubs that seem to take every last bit of nourishment. A most difficult spot. Yet those

Crocuses flower thickly year after year, increase in number, seed themselves on the bank and even in a gravel path and the flowers are really a fine size. It could be that they get a fair amount of sunbaking in summer; it could be they appreciate the complete dryness of summer when the shrubs take up all the moisture; it could be something I cannot guess. After all we can't understand everything.

One of my little tricks is to go down to the bottom of the garden on a cold day in early March, carefully pick half a dozen Crocus buds that are just coming through, bring them in and put them in a tiny vase or egg cup in a warm room. Inside an hour they are full out, as wide as little saucers, white, yellow, purple as rich as the robe of a Caesar.

On a day when you wonder if spring will *ever* come it is a cheerful sight.

For the small garden where there are no rough banks or orchards or areas where grass can remain uncut until late I think the best place for the Crocuses is the front of the border, a kind of ribbon edging to a bed. Better have one or two corms than none at all, and if they are suited they will increase, but with Crocuses the more the merrier, though if you are planting them for the first time space them out well or they will get crowded too soon.

Crocuses have been cultivated plants for thousands of years and many herbalists and doctors of ancient times, and of many races, made use of it in medicines. *Crocus sativus* became famous as a flavouring (saffron cake) and a dye. It seems to have reached England early in the fourteenth century and was first grown at Walden in Essex which became so famed for it that its name became Saffron Walden, though Culpeper in his herbal was still calling it Walden more than three centuries later. The story of how the roots reached this Essex village was first told by Hakluyt and I think will bear repeating: 'It is reported at Saffron Walden that a Pilgrim, proposing to do good to his countrey, stole an head of saffron, and hid the same in his Palmer's staffe, which he had made hollow before of purpose, and so he brought the root into this realme with venture of his life; for if he had bene taken, by the law of the countrey from whence it came, he had died for the fact.'

I suppose saffron must still be obtainable but there are easier and cheaper flavourings and dyes. It took the dried stigmas of more than four thousand flowers to yield an ounce so it can never have been very cheap. Gerard and Parkinson grew it and Culpeper managed half a page, which was moderate for him, of medical uses. It was good for the heart: 'It is an Herb of the Sun, and under the Lion, and therefore you need not demand a reason why it strengthens the Heart so exceedingly.' For some strange reason it made people laugh and Bacon said 'it maketh the English sprightly'. Another herbal related that a woman of Trent was 'almost shaken to pieces with laughing immoderately for a space of three Hours, which was occasioned by her taking too much Saffron.'

So beware! A good laugh is fine—but three hours non-stop . . . !

THE SNOWDROP

There are only three main species of Snowdrop that I know of but with variations on these there are about a score. Since the bulb catalogues rarely have as many as half a dozen the information is given merely as a point of interest. To me there are two: singles and doubles. For singles it is worth writing to a good nursery and buying *Galanthus elwesii* (Galanthus means milk flower) which is a large substantial bloom, said to be the largest, though *G. nivalis,* our native flower has given some quite imposing varieties in recent years. The Snowdrop is generally included in any book on British wild flowers. Some say it is not a native but was introduced by the Romans, by the Crusaders, by monks . . . you may take your choice. And I have heard that it grows wild only near the sites of monasteries. Certainly the one spot where I have seen it in the woods so thickly that you might imagine snow was on the ground is opposite a hill on which are fragments of ruins. I was told it had been a castle but not with much conviction: it could have as well been a small monastic house. This is down by the sea at St Ishmaels in south Pembrokeshire, as beautiful and romantic a beach as you are likely to find anywhere—and so off the map that very few people *are* likely to find it.

Some gardeners think of the winter Aconite as the first flower of spring but I have never done much with those pleasant little yellow flowers and the shooting of the Snowdrop leaves is my own particular signal that spring, even if far away, will come in time. It is strange that no country name compares Snowdrops with bells for they are bell-like as they swing to and fro. How they do swing on those delicate threads which connect flower to stem. You'd think they would be torn off. But they can stand any gale that blows. They yield to the wind rather than oppose it. A tree may be blown down in the night but never a single Snowdrop head is blown off. Their strength is that they know when to give in. There is a moral in that somewhere.

But country people give familiar names to flowers they like and perhaps they never liked the Snowdrop overmuch. I know there were superstitions about them in the village where I grew up and they were unpleasant ones. If I remember rightly it was unlucky to bring them into the house too early in the year. They said the same thing about Primroses and though I reckon to be sensible and fairly rational now, I still have a slight uneasiness about picking precocious Snowdrops before February or Primroses before March. My own family was moderately well educated but all my spare time was spent among country folk, many of whom had hardly gone outside their own parishes and quite a few of them could not read or write. But they had their own lore and I absorbed a lot of it.

One superstition about Snowdrops was that if you brought the early bloom into the house the eggs under the sitting hens would not hatch.

There was a legend that the flowers were made from snow-flakes by an angel to comfort Eve when she was turned out of the Garden of Eden. It was a sort of symbol of better things to come.

The flower was dedicated to the Virgin. Traditionally it flowered on Candlemas Day, February 2, that being the day on which She took Jesus to present Him in the Temple. So the flowers in medieval times were called Fair Maids of February. Curiously I cannot find that either Chaucer or Shakespeare, who between them surely knew every flower that grew, even mentioned them, but it is possible they did under another name, and Gerard and Parkinson and other early writers knew and grew them and it was described by Theophrastus about three hundred years before Christ.

It was the custom in olden days to remove the Virgin's picture from the altars of churches at Candlemas and strew Snowdrops in their place.

Plant the bulbs where you will but remember one thing: if you plant them in some out of the way spot you may never see the flowers if the weather turns rough and wet and cold when they are out. The best places are in spots where they cannot fail to catch the eye when you look out of windows, and when you go to and fro on your lawful occasions. They are not bulbs to be given beds to themselves but they will flourish under trees, under shrubs, and in places where later plants are growing. The singles are lovely but the doubles are substantial and make a more conspicuous show. They have a delightful scent and they grow admirably in pots and bowls indoors though conditions should be cool for they do not take kindly to forcing. If you happen to keep hens and like to hatch out your own chicks under a hen in the way nature intended, perhaps you had better leave them outdoors. I'm not saying the risk of a poor hatch is great but you have been warned!

Chapter 10: OTHER SPRING BULBS

There are quite a few more bulbs that can be planted in autumn to flower in spring, but most of them have some drawback, the chief ones being that they are either difficult to grow or are not nearly as pretty as the familiar ones. A few are tender and usually die out except in the very warmest gardens.

The three I like best are Muscari, Scilla and Chionodoxa. They are I believe related to each other and to the Hyacinth.

Muscari have been grown in this country for hundreds of years. There are more than 50 species but, though some of the early gardeners and herbalists grew quite a number of them only a few of the best are on sale today. Just as well, too, for the differences between many are so slight as not to matter to the gardener. About the best is *M. armeniacum;* it is generally called Grape Hyacinth and most gardeners are familiar with the six inch stem with the little bells clustered for an inch or so down the top of the stem. The flowers have a sweet scent, a fact often unrecognised because the bulbs are generally planted far below nose level. I have a white variety, probably *M. azureum album* but it is much smaller than the blue one. The only other I have grown you may find in the lists as *M. comosum plumosum,* in which the sterile flowers have been changed into long filaments, so that the spike has a bottle-brush appearance. I would say it is more curious than beautiful.

The only fault in this delightful plant is that it increases at such a rate as to threaten to choke out less vigorous plants. Parkinson wrote of this prodigality in his *Paradisus* when he said 'it will quickly choke a ground, if it be suffered long in it. For which cause, men doe cast it into some bye-corner . . . or cast it out of the garden quite.'

Personally I have no complaint at all. I have given it a few generous pockets in the rock garden and those drifts of almost solid blue each spring are a very cheering sight. And if they increase . . . well I suppose when I first planted Muscari the bulbs cost a penny each; at the moment of writing they are from sixpence to a shilling each, and say, a ninepenny bulb that produces lots more ninepenny bulbs in a short time does not seem much to grumble about.

SCILLA

The best known Scilla is *Scilla siberica*, the Squill, a Bluebell a few inches tall, that flowers in early spring. It is a pretty little thing and makes fine drifts of blue when planted in a rockery bed, but it is as well to aim at having it at eye level so that you get its full value. I tend to give advice like that because my own rock garden is part dry wall, part terraced bed and I have no difficulty in placing flowers where I can look them in the eye. But the Scilla is easy in pots or containers such as window boxes. It is a good plan to put them fairly thickly, since unlike Muscari they do not increase very fast from offsets. They do seed themselves freely but the seedlings take a year or two to reach flowering size. There is a white form but I much prefer the blue. Scillas come from most parts of the world except the tropics but the African species, not easy to obtain anyhow, are suitable only for the Alpine house.

While on the subject of Scillas it is worth mentioning a related bulb, the Puschkinia which is a pale blue. I have grown these and in appearance there is not much difference between them and the Squills, so unless you particularly want the species I think the money would be better spent in getting a really imposing drift of Scillas, or Jacinths as Tudor gardeners called them.

CHIONODOXA

The Chionodoxa is another member of the Bluebell family, but it only came into cultivation in the late nineteenth century. It comes from Turkey, or at least the first specimens did, and since it was found there growing on a 4,000 foot mountainside in great profusion it seems rather strange that it was not noticed much earlier, particularly as the Turks at that time were very good gardeners. But one does tend to overlook one's weeds; is there an Englishman who would praise a bank aflame with golden Dandelions?

The common name of this flower is Glory of the Snow and that is what the Latin name (Greek really) means. I don't know that it has ever dyed the snow in our own garden (and we get our share at times) but presumably it could and would. I think it is rather prettier than the Scilla for where the latter hangs its blooms bell-fashion the Chionodoxa looks up at you, open-flowered. It will grow anywhere, even in a path as some of my self-sown seedlings do, and seems to spread by seed. As well as the blue varieties there is a pink form and a white, but I am fairly satisfied with the blue: a good eyeful of blue in spring, when there are already whites and yellows to be seen, is well worth having.

There are other spring bulbs, some worth having, some not, and some that are too temperamental or tender to bother with. But the Erythronium deserves a place and though really easy and common most gardeners have to ask what it is. The common name is Dog's Tooth Violet—goodness knows why because they resemble neither dog's teeth nor Violets. They come from North America and Japan and were introduced, and it is believed, first grown by de l'Obel, a botanist and gardener who settled in this country about 1584. The Lobelia is named after him. Most of the early gardeners and herbalists grew the plant. They had an idea that it was the Satyricon of Dioscorides. Now the Satyricon (after the over-amorous satyrs) was the source of a famous aphrodisiac, so goodness knows what concoctions were made from Erythronium roots—and swallowed. 'Wee have had from Virginia a roote sent unto us, that wee might well judge, by the forme and colour thereof, being dry, to be either the roote of this, or of an Orchis, which the naturall people holde not onely to be singular to produce lust.' Let's hope it did the patients good: a little faith is a great help.

These flowers are said to need shade and moist well-drained soil. My own little colony grows in full sun on a heavy clay that bakes like a brick in summer—when we get a summer—so I would classify it as an easy plant. The leaves are attractively mottled and slugs will eat the flowers unless steps are taken to stop them. Slug pellets are useful but a thin ring of permanganate of potash crystals round the plant is even better. The species most grown is *Erythronium dens-canis* but bulb merchants will have up to half a dozen other species or varieties to choose from.

ANEMONE

It would be unforgivable to leave the Anemone out of the bulb list (it grows from a tuber not a bulb) though it can be sown, and will flower, at almost any time of the year.

The story goes that a Bishop of Pisa by the name of Umberto, thought up the idea that ships carrying Crusaders to the Holy Land should bring back soil as ballast. This sacred soil was spread over the Campo Santo in Pisa and the next spring the Campo was covered with scarlet flowers which the people thought must have sprung from the blood of martyrs. It was, naturally, regarded as a miracle and in time pilgrims carried the plants and seeds of *Anemone coronaria* all over Europe. This may be weak from a garden historian's point of view, but as a legend it seems to me to rank fairly high—and is not entirely impossible as fact.

Those who pick our best stories to pieces point out that Anemones grow in most Mediterranean countries; it was popular among Greeks and Romans for their garlands; it sprang from the tears Venus shed over Adonis. Pliny said the first Anemone of spring was a charm against illness—this superstition lasted for centuries and girls sewed the first spring Anemone into the doublets of their lovers when they went to the wars.

The most commonly planted are either the de Caens or the St Brigids, both colourful, both pretty. If they are sown in autumn in a warm well-drained soil they flower in spring. If they are planted in spring they will flower their first season in summer but afterwards, like the rest of the family, in spring. Sometimes they do not flower at all. I have a suspicion that some of those we buy cheaply on the stalls have had the life dried out of them. They often need some kind warm spot for I have had failures in parts of my cold hillside garden while the ones I see in Herefordshire gardens a few hundred feet lower and a good many degrees warmer, flower like rainbows in the spring sunshine.

Chrysanthemum maximum, Esther Reed. One of the best of the large Daisies

Rosa Centifolia, the Cabbage Rose. This particular plant is at least 100 years old, probably much more

Above: Russell Lupins. Colourful summer border flowers
Below: Rosa gallica: one of the most beautiful shrub roses

Above: Aquilegia, or Columbines. A group of the long-spurred variety
Below: Rambler Rose, Dr van Fleet, flesh-pink and scented

The Garden Path. Border flowers below and a rock bank above,
in high summer

Our own woodland Anemone *A. nemorosa* is no mean flower and that grows very reliably, and in a spare corner of the garden develops a larger bloom than it does in the wild. The Pasque Flower, *A. pulsatilla,* is also a native, though a rare one, and is the plant used to dye Easter Eggs. The household accounts of Edward I relate that four hundred eggs were dyed by it for one of the Easter court festivals. I once raised a very fine colony from seed and the downy purple blooms were a great joy.

A. hepatica is said to be one of those flowers you had to wait for and Neil Lyons, a well-known writer of short stories, had a pathetic tale of an old man, pushed from pillar to post who insisted on taking his 'patikews' with him. I can't remember the end of the tale and I can't find the book but I have an idea they flowered at last when the old chap was dying.

The Father of English Botany, William Turner, said of Hepaticas 'this herbe is good for the liver, and specially for the liver of new married yong men, which are desyrous of childer.'

A. blanda comes from the Near East and is an easy flower, of great charm, in many shades of blue, pink and white, but I think my own favourite is the closely related blue *A. appenina.* I saw this many years ago, a great spring drift of it in an old and rather neglected rock garden in a famous but equally neglected house in the Welsh-English border. I thought I had never seen anything so lovely (I had, of course, but you know how these things go to your head) and I have been growing it (not in such quantities) ever since. It seems quite easy anywhere in the garden. A garden shop with a bowl of the tubers on the counter can charm a few shillings out of my pocket any time.

One other Anemone must be mentioned. This is the border plant *A. japonica,* not really Japanese but a native of China, introduced from Japan by Robert Fortune about 1844. This is a great cottage plant and nowhere have I seen it flourish more than in those gardens in Devon and Cornwall. I have had some pretty fine groups myself but only where the soil has been warm and well-drained, and since it grew like a weed in the garden of our home in south Pembrokeshire it is probably not at its best in cold areas or in heavy soil. In some gardens I have seen a variety in a soft, lavender pink, but there is no white flower that can rival the pure white Japanese Anemone. It takes quite a time to settle down after transplanting and in some gardens may take so long that the gardener's patience is taxed. But it is worth waiting for.

Some are very fond of flowers which other gardeners consider weeds so it ill becomes one who admires (in their proper places) Celandines and Dandelions to condemn anything out of hand.

Alliums are Onions. Or at least they are members of the Onion family. They were known to and grown by the early Elizabethans, and Spenser has a fairly well-known couplet.

> 'Sweet is the rose, but grows upon the brere,
> And sweet is moly, but his root is ill.'

Which I suppose was his way of moralising that there is a drawback to everything.

Moly is *Allium moly,* Golden Garlic, a pretty yellow flower, but, as Spenser says, in the bulb anyhow, smells horrible. A number of them (Alliums) were grown in Tudor gardens and I imagine they were more valuable in charms and physics than in bouquets. Gerard was scornful about the magic: 'As for repeating of foolish and vaine figments, the conjuring of witches and magician's enchantments, which have been attributed unto those herbes, I leave them to such as had rather plaie with shadowes, than bestow their wits about profitable and serious matters.'

Fair enough, but Gerard, interesting writer though he was, could hand out some pretty tall yarns on occasion so it did not behove him to be too scornful of others who did likewise.

There were many Molys or Alliums and some, Garlic, for instance, undoubtedly have useful medicinal qualities. As for the magic it was the juice of Moly that enabled Circe to turn the companions of Ulysses into pigs.

For planting I find my bulb merchant has 18 species for sale. Some, I guess, are not worth garden space, but A. *moly* is yellow and pretty, and A. *ostrowskianum* is purple and also pretty. Most of the roots are edible, if not always palatable; others are so objectionable in flavour that I doubt if anybody has experimented far enough to prove if they are poisonous as well.

I have grown Brodiaeas which produced heads of blue flowers but though they are said to be hardy mine died out quickly and

I was not sufficiently attracted to plant any more. What I have found among the less familiar bulbs, Camassia, Ixias, Sparaxis and so on is that they are slightly tender in warm gardens and hopelessly so in cold ones.

There is a spring-flowering Colchicum, *C. luteum,* which is quite a pretty flower (so it ought to be with bulbs at three or four shillings each) but I think *C. autumnale,* the Autumn Crocus (which is not a lot cheaper) more worth growing. There are a few species and varieties of this, one white, and they are very pretty. The flower comes before the leaf, and that I know is rather poisonous.

Some confusion has arisen because there is an autumn-flowering Crocus that *is* a Crocus, so to order by name can lead to stocking up with the wrong plants. Price is a good guide to getting the right ones for the true Crocuses seldom cost more than a few pence.

Sternbergias are also worth planting for autumn flowers. They are Crocus-like in appearance but yellow.

There are about a dozen hardy Cyclamen, some flowering in autumn and some in spring. These little corms are excellent for naturalising where the soil suits them. They prosper in light shade, rich soil and need shallow planting. In time the corms grow as wide as a small saucer and produce an amazing number of the tiny pink or purple flowers. A good species for autumn is *C. europaeum* while for spring I think *C. coum* is about the best. In olden days it was used to make a medicine to help in childbirth and so powerful it was in this respect that Gerard fenced his in so that no pregnant woman should stand over them and have a miscarriage! It was Gerard also who said 'it is reported to be a good amorous medicine to make one in love, if it be inwardly taken.'

Beverley Nichols in *Down the Garden Path* was full of praise for the Winter Aconite *Eranthis hyemalis* but after trying a few I was not impressed. Perhaps I was prejudiced against 'these venemous and naughtie hearbs' because I read that it is the most deadly of all poisonous plants. Some writers identified it with the Aconite of classical literature which was the brew Medea offered

to Theseus. Luckily for him he threw it on the ground and
it seethed and sizzled until the marble cracked. They say even
rabbits will not touch it.

There are two Fritillaries, very different from each other and
very different also in price. The expensive one is *Fritillaria im-
perialis*, the Crown Imperial, a Persian plant with a long history,
some legends but not very impressive ones, and associations
with many important botanists and gardeners. Some liked it. Parkinson admired its 'stately beautifulness', while others thought
them poor things and one said they were 'of a Colour like to that
of a boiled Lobster' which, however much you like lobster can
hardly be called a compliment.

The other is the Snake's head Lily, *F. meleagris*. These are
fairly cheap but better see one or a picture of one before you buy
because again opinion is divided as to their garden worth.
Judgements on this vary from Parkinson who said it was 'a wonderful grace and ornament for a garden' to V. Sackville West who
said it was a sinister little flower. They are certainly unusual, but
would not appeal to everyone. Though grown in gardens and
introduced from various countries the Snake's head is a rare native.

Most of the country names for it verge on the uncomplimen-
tary—Sullen Lady—or are frankly insulting—Madame Ugly. It
was associated with leprosy because the bells were thought to
resemble the bells lepers had to carry with them, and they have
been called Lazar Bells.

Both the Fritillaries are easy to cultivate. The bulbs of Crown
Imperials need deep planting, say 7 inches in rich soil. Snake's
heads, which will grow under trees, also need good soil, good
drainage and should be planted 4 inches deep.

The Irises deserve at least a chapter to themselves, and in fact,
a number of books have been devoted to them. The ones that
grow in the border from rhizomes, the bearded Irises, are,
though fairly easy, looked on as specialists' flowers, but considered here as bulbs the most familiar are the three hybrids of *Iris
xiphium* known as Dutch, English and Spanish Irises. The only
difference between them as far as I can see is that they flower a

week or two apart in that order. They are lovely flowers and are available in many shades, mainly purple, yellow and white. In warm gardens they seem to be easy and reliable, coming up freely year after year; but in cold gardens with heavy soils they cannot be relied on and I have had them die out especially after cold wet winters. Where the soil is light and warm, planting in September and October is quite in order but in my own garden I prefer to put them in some time during early spring.

A delightful little winter-flowering Iris is *I. reticulata* but I always grow these in pots. Gardeners in more kindly climates seem to have no difficulty in getting them into flower by or before March in sheltered pockets in the rock garden. The flowers are in shades of purple and are fragrant.

After reticulatas I am afraid we are back on ground trodden only by Iris experts. There are many species ranging from not-too-hard-to-grow to downright difficult. Many are so lovely that they are worth all the trouble their admirers go to, but I've reached the stage when in the words of the Elizabethan poet, George Wither,

> 'If she be not fair for me
> What care I how fair she be.'

There are other bulbs for spring flowering besides the ones I have mentioned in this chapter, but I want this book to be about popular plants and I do not see how a plant can become really popular if it is tender or unreliable. So I have left out such as outdoor Freesias or Ixias or Nerines or the giant Ranunculas and if you fancy any of these or others you can easily find a bulb merchant who will sell you some. But you may need to take pains with them. For example I have seen Arum Lilies flourishing like weeds in a Pembrokeshire garden, and once I was shown over the garden of the Master of St Cross at Winchester and there I saw a huge colony of these lovely things planted in the pool that used to be the fish pond of the monks.

So all things are possible—well, nearly all!

But one parting suggestion (from this chapter) I will give. If there is a bit of rough ground spare, a space under shrubs or in an orchard, an awkward corner, plant a good colony of Star of Bethlehem (Ornithogalum). Plant in autumn and the reward, which will appear in spring, and with luck in all the springs to come, will be worth much more than the trouble taken.

Chapter 11: BULBS TO PLANT
IN SPRING

In the garden we use the term 'bulb' very loosely since some of our so-called bulbs, which are buds, are corms or thickened stems, while others may be tubers (underground stem food stores) or rhizomes, also underground stems.

Nearly all the summer plants grown from these are tender to a greater or lesser degree. With some of them gardeners feel the little trouble they give is worth while so there are Gladioli and Begonias and Dahlias in every garden though it may be necessary to take up and store the roots. Other plants in this class are for enthusiasts only and so in the majority of gardens you will not find Crinums or Nerines or Arums.

The most popular of the summer bulbs is the Gladiolus, so named because of the sword-shaped leaves. There was once a common name, Corn-flag, but it has been little used; in fact if it is used at all now it has been for some other plant such as one of the wild Irises. There is supposed to be a rare English native Gladiolus growing somewhere in Hampshire but I have never seen it. The sixteenth century gardener, Henry Lyte calls it Coarne Flag or Coarne-gladdyn and Gladdon is now the common name for *Iris foetidissima* so there may be some confusion due to the similarity of the leaves. Gerard seems to have grown it. My edition of his herbal, a reprint, has no illustration but the description of the flowers undoubtedly refers to the Gladiolus. He also uses the name Corne-Flag and Corne-Gladdin. He said it was an Italian plant; there are a few European species, which have been known in gardens for a long time. He said 'the cods with the seed dried and beaten into pouder and drunk in Goats milke or Asses milk, presently taketh away the paine of the Colique.'

Various species of Gladiolus seem to have been popular at least since Gerard's days but there were not many kinds to choose from. Older gardeners will probably remember some of the varieties, smallish-flowered compared with the moderns, that lasted through from Victorian gardens. These if lifted had long strings of exhausted corms like strings of beads. Gladiolus roots conveniently draw down the corms to their correct depth so that the old ones descend further and further. Presumably when colonies were left alone for a long time the oldest ones must have rotted.

As time went on more and more species were introduced, some specially well-coloured from Africa, and it was those smart gardeners the Dutch, with some competition from Belgium, who started hybridising in a big way. Nowadays, of course, the corms are being grown in enormous numbers. Someone told me that more Gladioli are sold now than any other bulbs. They come in all colours, though I doubt if there is a true blue, and while a bed in a garden is vivid enough, a field full of a nurseryman's treasures is enough to dazzle anybody.

I am afraid that there is a slight danger, only a slight one, but it exists, that the hybridist may overdo the two virtues of brilliant colour and enormous size of bloom. You *can* have too much of anything, good or bad, and I have noticed two pointers that indicate that size is not all the gardener wants in his garden.

One was the popularity some years ago of *G. primulinus*. This was introduced about the end of the last century by Fox, the engineer who was responsible for the bridge across the Zambesi near the Victoria Falls. He found the flower growing near the waterfall. It was fairly small and the top petal was rather like a canopy; it protected the organs of the flower from mist and drifting spray. The hybridists used it to develop new colours, mainly yellow shades, but in time the flower became popular in its own right among gardeners who were getting tired of the giants that all the time grew taller and taller.

The second occasion I seemed to smell rebellion was a few years ago when an even smaller type was developed. These were named Butterfly Gladioli. Their flowers are more frilled than the larger types, and of course they are almost miniatures by comparison. A difficulty here is that with good cultivation the stems tend to grow taller, the flowers larger; on the other hand if they are not well cultivated they are not as attractive.

It's a hard world, my masters.

All the same they are very much worth growing: if you like Gladioli and are getting a bit tired of the weight of the giants they are almost indispensable.

Some lucky gardeners in the south are able to plant Gladioli and forget all about them. I think even in their gardens the corms will deteriorate in time. In my own garden I have one purple stalwart in a sunny spot under the greenhouse wall that has been coming up year after year for half a dozen years. It's a struggle I think but it does try.

In most gardens the corms must be planted in spring. They can have a bed to themselves or they can be planted in single rows which is a very convenient way when support is needed—as it always is. My own method is to plant in circular groups with not more than a dozen in each, in the mixed border. According to the season they can be planted from the end of February onwards. In cold districts it is doubtful if there is much advantage in early planting because neither roots nor shoots will start while the temperature is very low. Planting can go on until about the end of May and by putting in a few at a time the flowers may be enjoyed over a long period. They like a deep well-drained soil, plenty of sun (when there is sun) and the soil should be reasonably rich. They flourished most when farmyard manure was plentiful but now that is so precious—and pricey—they manage very well with a good general fertiliser. This should be dug into the soil and mixed in thoroughly and quite deeply, some time before planting.

In soils that are at all on the heavy side the sites should be dug out, bowl shaped, large or small according to the number of corms to be used, and the bottom liberally spread with coarse sand. The corms are spaced on this, roughly 9 inches apart (less for the Butterfly type) and covered with about 4 inches of soil. Deep planting is a disadvantage because it takes so long for the heat of our intermittent sunshine to warm the soil.

So the planting routine goes roughly like this.

A good depth of well dug, rich soil

A thick layer of sand

The corms

4 inches of top soil

Quite a sandwich. But if I may adapt that saying 'some chicken; some neck!' I would add 'Some sandwich, some flower!'

Staking is tiresome but essential. If the plants are not staked they will at the best lean drunkenly in all directions; at worst be blown flat.

You can put a cane to each individual plant but in beds, or in rows the simplest method is to put in strong stakes, tie strong cord or wire from stake to stake and the stems to the wires. For small groups you can use bushy sticks round each group, but for these I use a ring of three or four canes, tie string round the canes, also some across the group from cane to cane.

I don't know what the big growers do, I've never noticed —nothing I expect—but we lesser mortals, like Addison's Sempronius must *deserve* success.

When the flowers are out you could think you had a rainbow in your garden, but the flowers have one nasty habit: they die. The lowest flower dies first, then the next up the stem, and the next . . . and so on. A Gladiolus bed full of dying blooms is a depressing sight so I regard it as a 'must' to go round them say twice a week and pull off the dead and fading flowers. Fortunately they pluck out as easily as feathers from a moulting hen.

When autumn comes gather up your stakes, dig up the Gladioli, tie them in bundles and hang them in any building to dry. In a month or so the leaves will have become brown and that is the time to twist the corms from the stems. At the same time twist the old corms off. Store the new corms in paper bags, in boxes or places where frost will not reach them. Polythene bags are not to be recommended unless you are prepared to inspect them regularly because there is always some moisture in corms and they might go mouldy.

That seems about the end of the programme and all you do is replant when spring comes round again. Incidentally many corms increase and you get two full-sized ones where you planted one.

There is just one other thing. When you clean the corms there are a lot of very small corms, about the size of peas or smaller, round each parent corm. These are known as spawn and every single one is capable of growing, in time, into a full-sized corm which will give a flower identical in colour to the parent.

To try to grow all these to full size would be enough to drive anyone mad—quite apart from the fact that the earth would in a few years be so packed with Gladioli that there would be no room on it for people (I can think of a wisecrack there but refrain!). But it is well worth picking out the largest of the spawn, say all as large as marbles, storing them dry in a glass jar and planting them in the garden in due course and growing them to flowering size. You have profit in that you will get a lot of new corms, and the fun of growing them. Most of the larger spawn will flower in three years time and some may manage it in two.

The Begonia could easily rival the Gladiolus in popularity if it were as reliable out-of-doors. But it is not. I'm not sure whether it is the soil or the climate but I have a suspicion that suitable soil is an important factor because I have seen beds flourishing in gaudy colour in some mighty chilly places.

Also, I know that Belgium is quickly building up an important Begonia industry. A few years ago I was given an introduction to one of the country's foremost growers of these corms and invited to visit his nurseries. It was in a village near Ghent and as I hunted round for the place I wanted I must have wandered into half a dozen small nurseries, thinking I'd found it. Every one was crammed with Begonias in flower. Now the Dutch Tulip fields make a colourful scene in spring. The Belgium fields, full of Begonias in August are not far behind for sheer vivid colour. I am not sure they are not, some of them, a little in front. The nursery I visited and went over seemed to have one field after another carpeted with oriental splendour. Of course the corms would be lifted before winter. But my point is this. Most of Belgium away from the Ardennes is flat. And when the wind blows cold over those plains it is *cold*. But as far as I could discover the Begonias did not suffer. So presumably if you have the right soil you can grow Begonias successfully out of doors.

Of course they were growing them in greenhouses also. There

must, in the whole area, have been acres of glass. In them the blooms were an enormous size and the colour was enough to blind you. My French and my host's English were about on a par so I still am not quite sure what the under-glass blooms were for but I think many were for seed. And in one house I know they were working at getting a scented strain. I was told that in a few years they would get it, but just then, though a few chosen plants had a pleasant smell, I would not say that there was exactly an overpowering perfume.

The technique, as it was explained to me was simple. Seed was sown under glass in early spring. The seedlings were pricked off and grown on in moderately warm houses until early summer when the young corms were planted out in the fields. They flowered but I think the flowers were picked and composted. In autumn the young corms were harvested and sold—largely exported. As I said above I did not get a complete understanding of *all* that was said but I had the impression that some corms were flowered twice before going on the market. That would be for gardeners who thought a larger corm meant finer flowers. Perhaps that is so but my impression was that you could get blooms just as fine, if not quite as many, from a small one year corm as from an older and larger one.

The soil used for pot plants was rich in humus, but well-drained. When available old manure was used but I think the thrifty Belgians did not waste much that could go on the compost heap. They also used pine needles in their compost heap. Now many English gardeners are suspicious of these. Some rake them up and burn them because of the oils (turpentine?) they say they contain. Well, Begonias, Belgian ones anyhow, *like* the oil in pine needles, and I expect ours would too if they got it.

Begonias for beds can be started in early spring by planting them in boxes, concave sides of the corms upwards. They must be kept warm and should never have enough heat to force them or draw them into plants with lanky stems. In early May, as soon as the danger of frost is over, they can be hardened off and be planted where they are to flower. They should, of course, never be mixed with tall plants. They do have a period of intense brilliant bloom but are very good for producing *some* flowers and colour right into autumn. They should be lifted, cleaned, and stored dry during the winter.

They make very good pot plants for flowering under glass and are not bad as house plants for short periods though in rooms it is often difficult to give them the humidity they enjoy.

There are other Begonias besides those that grow from corms and they could be mentioned briefly here.

B. semperflorens is a fibrous rooted kind that is used widely for summer bedding. This grows some 9 to 12 inches high and has a very long flowering period. Most colours are available except blue. Since all Begonias are half-hardy they are started off, as seedlings or rooted cuttings, under glass in spring.

Begonia Gloire de Lorraine is the popular winter-flowering hybrid. It is raised from cuttings in spring and potted finally in pots anything from 5 to 7 inches. In the larger pots they can give a very fine display from October until March and they are happy in a temperature between 55 and 60 degrees. This plant is much less common since foliage house plants became so popular but it is really a much more beautiful thing than many of the drab and dull subjects to which housewives have been giving their affections. There are by the way other winter flowering varieties but Gloire de Lorraine is the best known.

Begonia Rex is the kind with ornamental leaves. They do have flowers, rather drab ones, but are grown entirely for the beauty of the leaves. They grow from rhizomes, short fleshy rootstocks, and apart from the fact that they appear to tolerate no frost at all, are as easy to grow as cabbages, and thrive anywhere in sun or in shade, in cool conditions or in warm ones. They like a peaty compost, and a lot of water in summer. They will, when suited, make very large plants, and if a start is made with a well-coloured leaf, make a fine show. The usual method of propagation is to detach a mature leaf, make knife cuts in the veins where they join and place it underside down on a pot or pan of sandy soil. Young plants form at the cuts. I have not been invariably successful with leaf propagation but I find it easy with my own solitary specimen to cut off chunks of rhizome in spring and root them separately in pots. This technique is popular among my friends who admire Begonia Rex but do not like the high prices sometimes asked for them.

B. coccinea is a fibrous-rooted kind and is an attractive plant about a foot high with pendulous flowers. There are named varieties in a choice of colour. Another pendulous species is *B. fuchsiodes,* but hybrids are more commonly grown than the species. *B. nitida* is a very small one only a few inches high, while *B. haageana* is tall with hairy leaves and trusses of white flowers. There are other species but most of them seem to be used mainly for hybridising.

The Hemerocallis is the Day Lily so called because the individual flowers last only about one day. Their saving grace is that there is a flower head with lots of buds, so actually the plants have a long flowering period. As with Gladioli it is as well to go over the plants occasionally and pull off the flowers that have faded. Some gardeners believe the Day Lilies are difficult to grow: they are not. They do sometimes take a season or two to become established but once they are, they flower very freely and the roots, in my garden anyhow, spread so quickly that they threaten everything around. They are strong growers too with graceful arching leaves and flower stems up to 3 feet high. The two commonest species are *H. flava* which is yellow, and *H. fulva* which is a deeper colour. Hybridising has been widely carried out in recent years and most people are now planting named varieties in colours ranging from a light yellow to some near-reds, and the Americans have some that are nearly purple.

That reluctance to flower freely in their first seasons has led to a mistaken idea that these plants need rich and special soils but again (unless I am gardening on exactly the mixture they need) my experience does not bear that out and they seem to me to grow anywhere in anything and in fact are good plants for difficult places.

In China the flower has been grown through many centuries and it was known as the Plant of Forgetfulness because it was said it caused loss of memory. For this reason there is a tradition that it would cure sorrow, so it would appear that there may be some sedative drug in the root. *H. esculenta* which may be the same as *H. fulva* is used in the east as a flavouring in cer-

tain dishes. I believe it is called gum tsoy. The plant was introduced to England about the beginning of the seventeenth
century and was known as Lily Asphodiles. It is a member of the
Lily family, to which also Asphodels belong so those early botanists were not so far out.

Rather similar in flower shape but much smaller both in flower
and leaf is the Alstroemeria or Peruvian Lily, but these belong
to the Amarallis family and are not Lilies at all, though like Day
Lilies they have blooms mainly in the yellow to orange shades.
They grow from tubers that look as if they were made out
of candle-wax. I tend to group those two plants together for here
again we have a plant that is considered not the easiest to grow
and again it survives in my garden in spite of very rough treatment. The only thing I notice that could be considered temperamental is that in shade it flowers shyly, sometimes not at all. But
the tubers are persistent here and are difficult to eradicate.

Alstroemerias are natives of South America and were brought
here about 1831 though seedlings seem to have been raised by
Linnaeus nearly a century earlier. Linnaeus had a white species
which as far as I have seen is not in the bulb lists.

Somebody told me that the leaves of Peruvian Lilies grow
upside-down and I went out into the garden and checked and
indeed it is true. Where they join the main stem the leaf stem
twists so what should be underneath looks up at the sun. There
must be a reason for such peculiar behaviour but that bit of information nobody has volunteered yet.

The best Alstroemerias to plant are Ligtu hybrids which were
introduced in the early 1930s. In these there is a slightly wider
range of colour than in my own A. *aurantiaca*.

Of the other summer bulbs most are tender and some can only
be grown in the greenhouse. I have grown Acidantheras in the
open but lost them because I was a little late lifting them for winter storing. They were rather pretty and graceful with tubular
scented flowers and leaves like those of Gladioli.

Montbretias, of course, are as tough as they come, but they get
crowded very quickly and when they are crowded they do not
flower freely. But a colony in full bloom is a cheerful, even fiery
sight. I think Crocosmias are taking their place. They are almost

identical in appearance but twice as large and the foliage is
sword-like and very handsome. Some people say it is tender but
my own district gets some notable frosts and the Crocosmias, so
far, do not seem to have suffered at all.

Galtonia candicans is the same as *Hyacinthus candicans* (although it is not a Hyacinth) cheap to buy, with handsome white
Hyacinth flowers on a stem at least 3 feet high. This comes from
South Africa and is reputedly tender but I have had a small
group in the garden for some years and they still grow and still
flower, though the flowers are less and smaller than they were
when the bulbs were younger. There are only a few species of
Galtonia and hybridising would probably produce some very
handsome plants and some beautiful flowers. It was named after
Francis Galton, a traveller in South-west Africa, who died
in 1911.

The Paeony has a reputation for being very difficult to establish. It makes me wonder if anyone ever has moved a plant, because I cannot anywhere find a reference to it that does not
describe it as growing from a root. This is curious because I believe the root is a tuber and that is why I end this chapter with a
paean, or hymn of praise to Paeon the Greek god of healing, from
whom the plant took its name. Only my paean is for *Paeony offi-
cinales.* I am the man who *did* move Paeonies with no trouble at
all. I was digging up and replanting a flower border which, much
as I like them, had far too many of these flowers in it. I replanted
some and threw the surplus on the compost heap. Later the compost went in a trench in which I was planting potatoes and I left
them where they were because I can always find someone who
would like a root of 'those old-fashioned red paeonies'. As it has
turned out nobody has begged them—my visitors are not generally interested in the potato patch—and the plants flower merrily
and with great abandon.

That's my garden to a T! Interlopers all over the place and
everything where it shouldn't be.

There are not many species of this flower, at least not in cultivation. The true Paeony is a small shrub, very beautiful but not
very easy. It was so highly valued in China where it had been
grown as long back as men could remember that though it was

known through paintings and travellers' tales nobody got a root out of the country and into ours until the end of the eighteenth century.

But, beautiful as the true Paeony is, since it is not easy to grow well, it is not common in our gardens.

The 'old-fashioned' Paeony, *P. officinalis, is* easy and *is* widely grown, though not perhaps as widely as it used to be when great clumps of it could be found in half the cottage gardens in the country. Its needs are simple—patience, while it settles itself in, plenty of room, and good, deep rich soil. It has one drawback: it has a comparatively short flowering period, say a month. On the other hand it is a handsome plant in its own right and a strong grower and for the man who does not want too much work in his garden a few groups will grow happily with no attention at all for a dozen years or more. I have some in my own garden that have been going strong for at least twenty. A little manure or fertiliser occasionally will ensure lots of flowers. And what flowers, rich in colour, sweet in scent (some people do not like this), generous in size. I put a ring of wire netting round my plants because the spring gales do such heavy blooms no good at all unless there is something to hold them up.

Most bulb merchants sell tubers with other colours besides red. There are white, and a lot of shades of pink. I have one with a ring of outer petals and a cluster of smaller, lighter coloured ones in the centre, but it may not be *P. officinalis.*

I will end my paean before it becomes ballad-length!

The plant has an enormous literature surrounding it. It was described at least four centuries before Christ and there were nearly enough superstitions about it to fill a book. Like the Mandrake it had to be uprooted by a dog, to which it would be attached by a string. It was used in medicines for the falling sickness, the early name for epilepsy; it was a charm against witchcraft; it was 'very effectual for such as in their sleep are troubled with the Disease called Ephialtes or Incubus: but we do commonly call it the Night-Mare.'

Heigh-ho, a lot of old rubbish! How much wiser are we than were our forefathers!

Or are we?

Chapter 12: THE DIANTHUS FAMILY

The most popular members of this large family are the various pinks and right at the front is the Border Carnation.

This is one of the real gems of the flower garden, colourful, beautiful and blessed with one of the pleasantest scents in the flower world.

And easy to grow.

Or is it? Think over all the gardens you know, all the gardens you have visited, the gardens of your friends you pass through casually or often, and count those in which you have seen a really good bed of first-class Carnations. I am not referring here to the odd bushy, unbudded clump that you often meet in a casual way, but a decent collection, every stem disbudded to one flower, every flower a triumph in size, shape and colour.

Perhaps it is not so easy to grow after all.

I fell in love with Carnations many years ago after seeing some really choice blooms in a friend's garden. He assured me that they were no trouble at all to grow, so at the next convenient birthday I managed to collect a small but very choice collection from a nursery that specialised in these flowers. I read all I could on the culture of the plants; went to some pains to give them the soil recommended and the treatment recommended. As a result I had a few quite pleasant flowers, but they were not at all out of the ordinary—certainly nothing like as good as those in my friend's garden—and really that is more or less the end of the story. I propagated all the plants from layers according to the book, but they made indifferent plants and gave indifferent results.

Where did I go wrong? Well, to start with I probably aimed too high. Had I been content with more modest results I might have had them. I think I was, with too little experience and knowledge, trying to get blooms that would make Show Winners remove their hats in reverence. My plants suffered from over-much care. It's a bit like courting (if my memory serves me right) you mustn't show you are *too* keen.

I used to think soil was the key factor. It is *one* factor but it is not the whole answer. An old classic on Carnations, *Carnations for Amateurs* by J. L. Gibson says 'I have seen Carnations grow-ing like weeds in the South of Spain, cooped up in hot-looking, wide-mouthed, earthen pots and in soil that looked like sun-wasted dust.' And then he goes on to say what marvellous flow-ers he has seen in Scotland 'where a drought is a matter almost of hours and minutes, and sunshine filters through chance chinks in the clouds.'

Well, I have learned a little since I first read Mr Gibson's book and I am fairly sure that the best soil for Carnations is perfectly drained, almost to the point of dryness; it must contain ample food but not of the heavy types such as leaf-mould or manure; some old manure is all right, but not in large quantities, while absolutely perfect drainage is essential. The plants like as much hot baking sun as they can get, though after that reference to Scotland it seems they will do without; and the general belief is that clay soils are unsuitable but a lot of lime (best in old mortar rubble or something like that) is always necessary.

Carnations can be grown well on clay soils but on those they should be grown in raised beds. The one thing that did surprise me in Mr Gibson's book is his statement that an open site is best: 'the carnation loves full sunshine and the free winds of heaven . . . there is no call whatever to choose a sheltered spot. Boreas blows as kindly on the Carnation as Zephyr.'

This is worth some experiments in gardens subject to much wind. Most plants curl up when the gales begin to blow.

If you are successful with the Border Carnations their culture is very simple. Spring planting is best and as flower stems appear they need some support. If you just want a few pleasant blooms for garden colour and vases there is little else to do; if you want superior flowers of a good size then disbud to one bud to a stem. If you don't mind straggly bushy do-as-you-like plants leave them alone and with luck they will go on year after year. If you want fresh young stock that may give a few flowers good enough for the local flower show you must raise new plants from cuttings, which seem to be difficult to root, or layers, which are easy. All you do is to select low stems in late summer, make a tiny slit at a leaf joint, peg to the ground and cover with light compost. When this forms roots—say by next spring—detach it from the parent—and there is your young plant.

Carnations are very old plants in cultivation. Pliny, who wrote in the first century A.D., said that they were discovered by the legions in Spain and following an already established Spanish custom they used them for flavouring wine. (This may account for an old English name, Sops-in-wine.) Some experts thought the Normans introduced them to our country, though I see no reason why the Romans should not have brought a few for they were great people for taking their plants with them. In any case we have quite a few members of the Dianthus family that are, so far as I can find out, true natives.

It is mentioned in much of our early literature. Chaucer called it 'clove-gilofre', to Skelton it was 'ieloffer', to Shakespeare, 'gillyvore'. Oh happy days when a man spelled as he wished! 'Swete and goodly Gely floures' wrote Barnaby Googe in 1577. And then the herbalist-botanists grew it, Turner, Gerard, Parkinson, Culpeper and each used the spelling that suited him best.

They all seem to agree in calling it Gillyflower though nowadays country people use that name for the Wallflower. Apparently the word came from the Arabic *quaranful* which means clove. In Greek that became *Karyphillon* and thence came the Latin *caryophyllum* which gives us the family name *caryophyllaceae*.

Cloves were used for flavouring wine but cloves were one of the precious spices of the ancients, so, as the Roman soldiers in Spain discovered, Carnations would serve the same purpose. Stocks, having a clove-like scent, in many people's minds became confused with Carnations.

Caryophyllum became the Italian *garofalo*, that in French turned into *giroflée* and so to the English 'gylofre'. By Gerard's time there were two Gillyflowers—Clove-gillofloures were Carnations; Stock-gillofloures were members of the Stock family and then the one member, Wallflower, took over.

Drayton wrote of 'the curious choice clove July-flower'. But July had nothing to do with it.

Pinks could be described as the poor man's Carnations, and indeed the poor man, once described by the ridiculous title of working man (aren't we all!) did a great deal in the development of the flower. It seems that the working men (using the title in its Victorian meaning) of different districts had each their own plants which they cultivated to a pitch of high perfection. I do not know which part grew leeks as thick as tree-trunks and great bloated gooseberries like cannon balls, but the Yorkshire miners went in for Pansies and the cotton workers loved their Auriculas. In the same way the lowlands of Scotland devoted themselves to Pinks. 'Not for these people the delights of village pub . . . it was the pink that gave them most satisfaction.'

I wouldn't have thought it went *quite* as far as that.

Somebody has described the early nineteenth century as the Golden Age of the Pink—which as Sam Weller said seems going it a bit strong, but in all countries certain flowers did become a craze at certain times, and many nurserymen did their share to supply a demand. Things never went quite as crazy with Pinks as they did in Holland during the Tulip mania, but certain plants were expensive and there were some that ran into guineas, which you would think would put them rather beyond the reach of 'working men'.

The plant got another boost when the late Montague Allwood started to take an interest in the Dianthus family. I do not know a great deal about Mr Allwood (I think he wrote an autobiography) but he devoted his life to these plants, and hybridised, and introduced new strains and crosses and so on. In my early gardening days the name Allwood was practically synonymous with Dianthus and probably three-quarters, maybe more, of the Carnations and Pinks and Sweet Williams that are grown in gardens owe something to the work he put in on them over many years.

By now the Pink has taken its place as a very pleasant garden flower. I would say, considering its merits, that it is under-planted rather than over-planted and many gardeners who would enjoy it have overlooked it.

It is easy. There are a few Alpine species, mostly rare, that are difficult to grow, but all the common or garden kinds give no difficulty at all. They like sun and they like a well-drained soil with plenty of lime in it, but they will also grow in quite heavy soil. One of the best edgings I ever had was in a bed in front of a sloping lawn. The soil was clay and all the moisture in the lawn (average rainfall 60 plus inches) drained right to the front of the border. But the Pinks lapped it up and thrived on it.

There was, and still is, twenty yards or so in the background a belt of pine trees. Perhaps *they* drank a good share of our plentiful rain. It is a passing thought. Still, that soil *was* horribly wet at times.

Pinks come in all sizes, shapes and colours; singles and doubles. Unless you have a particular fancy, as good a way as any of getting a collection is to sow a packet of seed. If you want the best get the best. However expensive it really must be *the best*. Raise your seedlings under glass, (for control: they are quite hardy) plant them out when ready and choose the ones you like to cultivate and increase. The probability is that you will like the lot.

Many Pinks are named varieties; they come and they go so I will not mention them here. But do not overlook Mrs Sinkins. This is the one most people think of as *the* Pink of old cottage gardens. It was raised by a master of Slough workhouse about 1870, and he named it after his wife. It has never lost its popularity and there is not much chance that the people of Slough at any rate will ever forget it because it is included in their Borough coat of arms.

The best position to grow Pinks? Anywhere and everywhere. Most people use them in the front of borders, or as edgings, but the very best place is on top of a dry wall. This, as the herbalist Culpeper was never tired of stating, is the voice of Dr Experience. You *may* enjoy the scent of the flowers at ground level on a warm humid day, you can hardly fail to get it, but if it is on a wall at nose level then you have only to incline your head gracefully and you get it in full. And it is so good that it is worth getting in full. Another method which makes it easy to reach the full aroma is to use it in window boxes.

When I come to think of it I am a bit short on Pinks myself at the moment. But my old jungle is bulging at the seams anyhow, and my difficulty is to keep things out rather than bring more in.

I have a thriving couple of plants of some unknown variety I collected in someone's garden. It is so easy to propagate Pinks: you just pull out, not off, a stem which will come away, as out of a socket at a leaf joint. Such cuttings are known as pipings. In a sandy soil they root freely.

There are still some of the old edging plants that were growing when I took over the garden.

I have not for years been without a few clumps of the Cheddar Pink, *D. caesius*. These are very easy to raise from seed and a packet will give you a wide variety of shapes, sizes and shades, having their strong perfume in common. I suppose it *is* a native wild plant, some of the wild flower books include it, but I have not seen it myself, even around Cheddar. Wild or cultivated, it certainly is one of the nicest flowers for rock gardens or edgings —or almost anywhere, if it comes to that.

My other constant Pink is *D. deltoides,* the Maiden Pink. It is a miniature, making a kind of spreading drift with stems a couple of inches high with bright rosy pink flowers about as big as a six-pence. It seeds itself fairly freely so does not need any special propagation. Though this one has no scent it is so colourful and pretty that room should be found for it on every rock garden. It is a wild flower over most of Europe, and though I have not come across it here I have seen some specially well-coloured specimens in the hilly country of Central France. I tried to collect some but it was the wrong time for plants and too early for seed.

As for the name, well it could be from the German Pinksten which means Pentecost at which season the plant was in flower.

Or it could be from 'pink' (as in pinking scissors) meaning to pierce, and referring to the pointed petals of some varieties.

Or it could be derived from the Celtic *pic* which means peak, again a reference to the shape of the petals.

Or, simplest of all, it could be named because it *is* pink, though Shakespeare used the word Carnation:

''A never could abide carnation; 'twas a colour he never liked.'

Anyhow that gives plenty of choice of name origin; for all I know there are others.

As well as the common garden varieties, with Mrs Sinkins, perhaps, just leading the Cheddar Pink, there are many Alpine species for the rock garden. Most of them are fairly easy but a few are not and the latter are mainly for Alpine specialists, who like rare and difficult things.

'The conserve made of the floures of the Clove Gillofloure and sugar, is exceeding cordiall, and wonderfully above measure doth comfort the heart, being eaten now and then.'

Chapter 13: THE PRIMULA FAMILY

This is an enormous family. There are about five hundred species, and when the hybrids and various garden forms are added there is such a host that it would take a lifetime to know them all and a garden as big as Hyde Park to accommodate them.

Of course only a comparatively small number is in cultivation. As with the Dianthus family there are many specialists' plants which most of us will probably never see, and probably never want to grow. Even among the easy species there are a lot that the average gardener does not bother about.

Very roughly speaking you can divide those available into two classes. One, like our native Primroses, the Cowslip, the Polyanthus, are mainly plants growing in ordinary, fair quality garden soil. The other class needs a lot of moisture, almost boggy conditions and indeed often are listed as Bog Primulas. I know to divide them in this way is simplification carried to the last degree, but allowing for the usual overlapping and cross-breeding of various kinds I think it can be considered a fair guide.

The name Primrose is a corruption of *primerole* which is Middle English, and seems to stem from the Latin *primula*. 'Rose' is apparently an error. In this family our own wild form is not inferior in beauty to any foreign kind. There is a belief that it will not grow in cultivation, that is to say in gardens, though the hybrids from it will. That gives a fair idea of my contrary plot for here it thrives, seeds itself, and has colonised itself with the greatest of ease. Curiously there are parts of the garden where it will not grow at all and transplant we ever so carefully the transplants vanish as though they had never been. But where it likes it likes and it comes up as easily in a gravel path as in some moist cool corner where its arrival is not so surprising.

In some spots in the garden it could be considered a weed—but it is a nice weed.

Many gardeners transplant a few hedgerow specimens, but mostly the Primroses found in gardens are the coloured hybrids. These can be raised easily from seed and some wonderful shades are often found. They need fairly rich moist ground and are good for edgings though perhaps are best suited in light shade. They are very good under shrubs but may not be long-lived if the soil is starved by shrub roots. The point is, as with the wild forms, you seldom can tell exactly where or why they thrive. Either they are almost embarrassingly healthy or they sulk and fade away. I suppose there is a reason for this behaviour but I do not know what it is.

There are double forms of *P. vulgaris,* our native flower. There was once a curious superstition that if you planted a Primrose 'upside down' double flowers would result. Perhaps if you could do such a thing it would work but the difficult part is how to 'plant' something upside down because if you stick flowers and leaves in the soil and have the roots waving about in the air, that can hardly be reckoned to be planting at all. There was also a belief, and this dates from the fifteenth century, that double flowers came if you transplanted often. Neither theory sounds very promising but double forms there are in the wild and when we were children we hunted hard for them, and often found them, in our Pembrokeshire hedgerows.

Cultivated forms of the double Primrose have been grown in gardens for centuries and some good varieties came from the south of Ireland, and still do, where the climate suited them very well. There was a craze for growing these named doubles at one time, but though it lasted a long time it died out at last probably because many of the plants faded away, for they were never the easy-to-grow plants that the singles were. Many are still available but mostly from Ireland and very few are offered by English nurseries. Someone sent me a collection as a present many years ago but though Primroses grow here so well they dwindled and died away in the end. I remember two we had in our garden when I was a child. One was pure white, the other lavender. So far as I can remember they grew very well and lasted, but even in the county of Primroses where banks and fields covered by the flowers in spring are a common sight, I think the double ones must have proved less accommodating.

The Cowslip, *P. veris* is another wild flower that seems to be found in particular districts. There were a few in the Pembroke-shire hedges, but the counties of the English-Welsh border are where I have seen them most. I have known Hereford fields literally yellow with them. Better for Cowslip wine than plants for the flower border, though.

But a hybrid between the Primrose and the Cowslip has given us one of our really notable, late spring flowers, the Polyanthus. This hybrid when found wild is, according to some botanists, the Oxlip but according to others the Oxlip is a true species. That is of academic interest only. John Evelyn mentions 'several Oxslips, or Polyanthus's' so the plants have been known and grown for a very long time. By the early nineteenth century they became, like Garden Pinks, what are called Florists' Flowers and the 'honest working men' (perhaps a few of the slippery customers also) were growing them to perfection. There would appear to have been certain standards set, rules to which the flower must conform, in the varieties Florists' Flowers that appeared from time to time. The Polyanthus was popular on the Continent especially in Holland but it was said that those raised by the artisans of Lancashire and Cheshire were much superior to anything the Dutch had to offer. Another area that went in for them in a big way was Ayrshire and Lanarkshire.

Again the British 'working' man kept his feet on the ground as far as prices were concerned, but anything around £1 was fairly common though that must have been a large sum to men who earned less, or not much more, per week. Eventually the craze burned itself out; it always has when silly rules about form and shape and colour and markings have been of more concern than the flowers themselves.

Yet the Polyanthus is still, unlike some Florists' Flowers, as popular as ever. It deserves to be for it is easy to cultivate, cheap when raised from seed, and makes our gardens gay in springtime.

Another Primula that had a very similar career was the Auricula. It is thought that this was introduced by the Huguenot refugees about 1570. Gerard was growing a number of varieties by 1597 and, as usual, he knew what it was good for. Mountaineers in Switzerland made a medicine of it for vertigo and so 'it preventeth the loss of their best joynts (I meane their neckes) if they take the roots hereof before they ascend the rocks or other high places.' Parkinson had about twenty kinds and sang their praises highly. Their popularity increased and there are records by successive authors of the numbers of varieties in cultivation and always the numbers increased. Prices were high, too; plants often cost as much as a guinea and there is an account of one belonging to Peter Egerton in Cheshire that was valued at £20. That was an enormous sum though I don't think it was mentioned whether it was Mr Egerton's valuation, or whether he could have actually sold it for so much.

The intensive cultivation of the flower by the weavers and miners of Lancashire and Cheshire started in the early nineteenth century in districts where Huguenots had settled. The more the working classes grew them the more they were neglected by the gentry. Some queer methods of cultivation were practised. 'Juicy pieces of meat are placed about the root, so that it may in some measure live on blood.' Well Blood manure is excellent stuff but that is rather a messy way of giving it. A man called Emmerton who lived at Barnet wrote a treatise on the Auricula. I have never seen it but apparently he concocted some disgusting mixtures in which to grow the plants. There is a story that he largely used goose dung and bought some geese to be sure of a supply, but the geese got out and ate all his plants.

I do not think there is a tremendous enthusiasm for them at the present time. A few years ago I idly picked up a packet of seeds in a shop and later I raised a good stock of plants which I put out in a terraced bed above a wall. They flourish, though I give them neither raw meat nor goose dung, but I can never be absolutely certain that I like them a lot. Some of the colours are pleasant but there are some queer brownish shades that are more unusual than attractive. I put one chocolate ringed one in a five-inch pot where it seems perfectly happy. I bring it into the greenhouse in autumn, its flowers come with great freedom, perhaps half a dozen of them, and then when it has finished, out it goes again.

A collection in a cool greenhouse could brighten the early spring days considerably.

We are not rich in members of the Primrose family in this country but the few we have are among the best. Apart from Primrose, Cowslip and Oxlip, if the last two are different, I think there is only one of note. For the rock garden it is a little gem. It is *P. farinosa*, the Bird's Eye Primrose about six inches high, with neat little heads of purple flowers. It seems to be common in a few localities in northern England but not anywhere else.

The rest of Europe is not very much richer in Primulas than we are. But during the latter half of the nineteenth century some beautiful species began to arrive from Asia. This was the Golden Age of the plant collectors and Northern India, or more properly south-eastern Asia, were their best hunting grounds. On the whole you can say the species they found and brought back, mostly as seed, divide very much as suggested earlier into those that like the damp cool shade and humus-rich soils and those that like boggy soil and lots of moisture. A few are difficult but the majority of those that have become popular are as easy as any other Primroses.

P. denticulata is familiar to most gardeners, being the lavender-coloured, ball-headed species that blooms in late spring and early summer. Colour is variable and if you grow a batch from seed you are almost certain to get a few with white flowers.

The people who have the best stock of Asiatic Primulas are the Alpine merchants and the water-garden nurseries. The former have most of the miniatures, and most of the difficult kinds; perhaps also the rare ones and some of these can be expensive. The water-garden people sell the ones for bog gardens. I don't think there are any that actually grow *in* water, but conditions are hardly ever too damp for them and sometimes they will manage in awkward spots. I was given some seed once of *P. japonica*, which is the purple candelabra species with the circles of purple Primrose-shape flowers growing ring above ring all up the stem. I had simply nowhere to put them and planted them in the end in about the most ghastly spot in my grounds—not even in the garden—a north-facing wall where an ash heap had been cleared away to make room for a garage. The soil I am sure was pure ash (but fairly old) and rather sour. I expected the plants to die but they flourished rather more colourfully than the green bay tree. Not only that, but they seeded themselves all over the place like Groundsel. I used to lift trowelsful of seedlings to give away to friends—who generally failed with them. It's the old Primrose story again. Neglect them and they come up everywhere; be polite and in a season or two they will fade away.

There are a number of candelabra species of Primula but I think *P. japonica* is about the best unless you are going in for the family in a big way.

Another good easy plant for damp cool places is the tall *P. florindae* which the collector Captain Kingdon-Ward discovered in 1924 and named after his wife Florence. This has the usual Primrose rosette of leaves—big ones—and tall stems of yellow scented Cowslip-heads but of course a lot larger. It is worth a place in any water-garden, or for that matter in any other if you can give it suitable conditions.

P. pulverulenta is much like *P. japonica,* and *P. sikkimensis* could be compared with *P. florindae.*

We will let our own Primrose have the last word.

'The roots of Primrose stamped and strained, and the juice sniffed into the nose with a quill or such like, purgeth the brain, and qualifiesh the pain of the megrim.'

A good mixed border will contain many scores of plants, but it is difficult to imagine one without a few Delphiniums, some really massive clumps of Lupins and, as summer wears on, the wide colourful drifts of Phlox.

The Delphinium is the one most likely to be missing. It is hardy enough, in all conscience, and it spreads quickly, so that a few plants can soon become a fine group, but slugs are so fond of it that if you are not careful you do not notice until too late that they are devouring the young crowns. This is curious because the plant belongs to the Ranunculacae, the Buttercup family, and nearly all of those are more or less poisonous. Turner writing in 1552 of one of the earliest species of Delphinium to be grown here said 'it is a very poisonous plant' and he said the powdered seeds were 'strewed on children's hair to destroy vermin'. There is a story that flies are not found on the leaves, but that may refer to a fairly near relation, Monkshood, one of the most deadly of plants. Anyhow, poisonous or not, the slugs' digestion seem to cope and I never noticed *their* corpses lying among the plants.

The earliest Delphiniums grown in this country were called Larkspur or something near that. 'It is Larkes spur, larkes heel, larkes toe, larkes claw and Monkshoode.' Nowadays Larkspur is the annual form. The name Delphinium was given by the ancient Greeks who thought the unopened bud had some resemblance to the head of a dolphin.

The development of the modern flower is comparatively recent. It has been grown for a long time, but without any ecstatic enthusiasm. The Kelway firm began to work on it around 1870 and Blackmore and Langdon took it up early in this century. But the really magnificent, breathtaking spires that you can see at flower shows today date from about the 1920s and 1930s. The plant breeders have done noble work. The modern flowers really are magnificent; their colours are pure and rich and the complete stems are as beautiful as they are tall.

Yet it is a curious thing—at least this is my opinion—that all the good work done on the plant could easily kill its popularity as a border flower. Maybe I am wrong, the Delphinium Society will know, but if you raise plants to such a pitch of perfection, the ordinary gardener will tend to fight shy of them.

I remember not so long ago that you would hardly see a herbaceous border that did not contain one or more groups of very nice Delphiniums. They were tall but not too tall; the individual flowers on the spikes were large but not too large and we weren't fussy about having perfect flowers of perfect shape. The plants were easy to support by a few canes and a length of string, and a bit of a breeze in the night did not have us shivering in our beds lest those towering stems should be brought low. The Delphinium was just a jolly nice border flower.

Now it is an aristocrat. We may all love a lord but we don't all want to be lords, nor have them for our buddies. We are content to admire from a distance.

Stuart Ogg in his book *Delphiniums for Everyone* starts off by saying the flower is 'the Queen of the Herbaceous Border'. A fair description, but then some of us are shy of Queens—and dynasties fall as quickly as they rise.

I hope I make my point. The pleasant ordinary groups of blue in the border are no more. It is the magnificence we admire at the Show or nothing. So generally it is nothing. Many lovely flowers have been toppled by kindness. A pity if the Delphinium experts overdo it.

If you want Delphiniums in your border decide where you will have them. Allow patches of generous proportions and dig them and manure them and get the soil in really good heart.

Now you may (I am only advising) do one of two things.

You can go to a specialist, somebody like Blackmore and Langdon, say, and closing your eyes to all the wonderful plants they will show you, ask them if they have some unnamed, unflowered seedlings they can sell you. Most of the specialists have these,

Above: Dorothy Perkins: the popular pink rambler as an informal hedge
Below: Alberic Barbier grew on a wall

Gladioli: large-flowered, primulinus and butterfly-type

A variety of Decorative Dahlias

A bed of orange-yellow African Marigolds

Above: Sunflowers: the old fashioned singles make a colourful, late summer display. *Below:* Polygonum affine, a pretty flower for late summer with rich brown leaves all winter

and, by the way (compared with the aristocrats), they are cheap.
Maybe someone will try to wither you with scorn; fancy refusing
something that won sixteen gold medals at Chelsea Flower Show
in favour of unknown dross that will probably have spikes only
four feet tall and individual flowers only as big as a pre-metric
florin instead of coffee-cup saucer size.

But stick to your guns. Buy your plants, put them in the prepared places, fight slugs away with slug pellets or permanganate
of potash, stake modestly in good time, and perhaps help the
florets with a little Blood manure. Then you will be rewarded
not by a lofty Queen staring down at you from a dizzy height,
but with a very, very pretty group of blue border flowers that
will help to keep your garden gay for a good deal of the summer.

The other thing you may do is to ask your expert for a packet
of his very best seed. It will not be cheap. At present prices it
may be anything between five and ten shillings, but remember
you may get a couple of dozen plants from it. Sow these seeds
about the end of spring. Grow the seedlings on very carefully
and again in the fullness of time plant on the prepared sites. In
the first year you will probably get one spire of very nice flowers
per plant; in subsequent years you will get lots and lots of them.
If anything that is definitely sub-standard appears, throw it away;
and if anything turns up so magnificent that it is obviously des-
tined to get all sorts of awards from the R.H.S. it might be as well
to throw that away also.

Temptation comes easily and as Sam Weller's father said, or
ought to have said, 'man is a veak wessel'.

And (in a quiet whisper) keep away from the Delphinium
Shows or the iron of discontent will enter your soul.

According to legend Ajax went mad from disappointment
when Hector's armour was given to Ulysses and not to him so he
stabbed himself. Rather a silly thing to do but, again according
to legend, it gave rise to a very nice flower for the annual Delphinium sprang from his blood.

According to all I ever learned Lupins do not grow well
in lime soils and they soon die out on heavy clays. I am not on
lime but as for clay, well if they don't like it they manage to put
up with it very well for I have had large groups flourishing in my

Christmas-pudd'n stuff for I should think at least the last twenty years and their shadow has not grown noticeably less, nor are the flower spikes smaller or shorter as summer succeeds summer.

Still there is no sense in giving any good plant less than the best we have so here is my own method of getting the gay colours of Lupins into the border.

To begin with, individual plants are not much good. If you want a show you must have a good group or many good groups according to the room you have to spare. You want something else, too—patience!

Prepare sites wherever you want them in the border but to be on the safe side do not add lime. You can put in any other enriching materials but there is no need to overdo this since Lupins are much happier where the soil is not over-rich.

Again there are two methods of stocking with plants. You can go to a good nursery and buy as many as you need or can afford. Buy Russell Lupins. You take them home and plant them but do not be surprised if they do not do very well in their first year.

My own way takes a little longer, is less expensive and I believe gives good results.

Buy a packet of the best Russell Lupin seeds. Sow this in rows in spring in light soil in some part of the garden, such as the vegetable plot, where they will not be intrusive but where you can keep an eye on them.

The seedlings must be left where they are and not be transplanted—yet.

In their second year each should produce a spike of flowers. Go over these, examining each one very carefully. You must choose now the strongest plants and, after studying the colours very carefully, pick the ones you really want in your garden. The ones you do *not* want (there won't be many from a packet of carefully selected seeds) you can either throw away or give away.

The plants you decide to keep can be planted in their places either in autumn in light warm ground, or in the next spring if the soil is heavy and apt to stay wet in winter. You should again get a good spike of flowers and could easily get two or three.

After that it is routine. You may need stakes and some string round some of the groups because Lupins can become very heavy when laden with summer rains. Also they topple when the winds blow. I try to grow them close enough to hold each other up, giving support only to the outer stems which have nothing to lean against. If the early spikes are cut off high on the stems as the flowers die they will be succeeded by more, though smaller ones. Sometimes the plants go on producing flower stems until autumn.

The first Lupins I ever grew were pretty but by modern standards they were quite modest in colour. Those who prefer their colours to be not too barbaric might try these old-fashioned types. I remember a bluish purple and a very pleasant pink and even when more gaudy colours came on the market I remained faithful to my old plants and swore they were better than any of the new ones.

But a lot of work went into developing the flower. George Russell, a jobbing gardener, decided somewhere about 1911 that the Lupin had great possibilities. He was sixty years old then but he got to work on hybridising and selecting. I understand he used *L. polyphyllus*, the border Lupin of the time and *L. arboreus*, the Tree Lupin which was introduced from California soon after 1792. It was discovered by Archibald Menzies who was the botanist in Captain Vancouver's expedition when he was looking for the so-much desired North-West Passage.

George Russell went on with his work for over twenty years before it began to yield the results he wanted, but when they came they were startling. Everybody is familiar with the brilliance of the modern Lupin. You would hardly find any of the pre-1911 flowers in any except old-established gardens today, but those who remember them will agree that the best modern strains are hardly the same flowers. And all due to the hard work and patience of one simple old jobbing gardener. I don't know if they still put his portrait on the packets of seeds, but it was familiar enough a few years ago. I don't think we shall forget his name.

The Tree Lupin is a delightful shrub and I have heard that in the places where it grows wild it makes a wonderful sight. As a rule the flowers are white or cream though I have had bushes in which there was a faintly discernible tinge of purple. It is not, in the average garden, very long-lived. After its American west-coast home it may find our winters a little discouraging. It is a good seaside shrub, though, and in light sandy soils in a sheltered place I have known specimens a score or more years old. In other and less favoured spots the best plan is to gather seed and have a few seedlings handy for replacements, because it really is worth growing and no shrub is more generous with its flowers.

There is a bit of a mystery about the edible qualities of Lupin seeds. The Romans are recorded as using the annual varieties as food, but there are also some references to their being so bitter as to be completely unpalatable. Parkinson recorded that they had been used for food but added that they had to be 'often watered (soaked?) to take away the bitterness'. Yet a writer in the early nineteenth century said 'there is no poisonous plant in this whole order except the seeds of Lupinus, with which the Hippopotamus is killed.'

Well, if they will poison a hippopotamus what would they do to us!

Incidentally, the information in that quoted sentence is wrong. Laburnum seeds are very poisonous indeed, dangerously so to children, and when I was very young I was warned against eating the seeds of Sweet Peas because *they* would poison me.

As I have mentioned before the country folk among whom I was brought up warned us off everything they were not sure of on the principle that you can't be too careful, so I am not a good guide on poisonous plants. There is, however, a bulletin on this subject published by the Ministry of Agriculture, and a very interesting one it is too.

As to the Pea family in general my own, quite personal, belief is that though several members were and are used commonly as food, both for man and beast, there is something in them all that —taken in large enough quantities—does not agree with our tummies. Peas and beans are excellent foods, but if they are eaten to excess they can cause very acute indigestion. Laburnum seeds are poisonous; Sweet Pea seeds may be, and in Lupins there is the bitterness, and I now recall that Virgil has left a record of it. Sheep feeding too freely on clover will die: wasn't it clover that killed Gabriel Oak's flock in *Far from the Madding Crowd?*

There may be a bitter drug in the seed of all the family that has not been discovered, or which nobody has tried to discover. Another thought: Lupinus is from the Greek *lupe* and that means *grief!*

There are many Phloxes and most of them invaluable, generally mat-forming, in the rock garden. But those all gardeners know well are the varieties of *P. decussata* which was once thought to be a hybrid though it now seems to be agreed that it is a species. The name was a bit of a mystery to me in my early gardening days because my neighbour who grew some very nice ones used the generic name as a plural, which made one stem of the flower a 'phlock' while three became 'phlocks'.

There may be many gardens where Phlox is not grown and I remember once I won First Prize in the local Flower Show for a dozen stems of Phlox. The fact that there was no other entry may have had something to do with my success. Some people find the heady scent, which is strongest in the evening, rather more than they like, though most gardeners enjoy it and so do the flies, bees, wasps and butterflies. It is easy to grow almost anywhere in any soil though if my own experience is anything to go by they do well in heavy ground. They grow in shade and I have some very healthy colonies under tall trees. It is doubtful if they would do as well if the shade were dense. Not the least virtue of the plant is that it comes out in late summer when the border, having lost the first glory of the Delphiniums and Lupins, is beginning to look a little jaded. Some years ago, apart from a dazzling white, colour was not a strong point, but a good deal of crossing has gone on and now you can have almost any gaudy tint, though there is not a yellow and not a really true blue.

The only place where the plant is a native is North America as far as I can discover. It got here in the early eighteenth century but seems to have made a rather pedestrian progress for a hundred years and more. In fact, it would not be far out to claim that the really good modern Phloxes are the work of Captain Symons-Jeune who many keen gardeners will remember both for his gardening and his garden writing. That is not to say that there were not *some* good colours before he got to work on them, nor that other keen breeders have not done their share of the work, but his part was such that his name comes first to mind when the plant is mentioned.

The best-known of the Campanula family are the Canterbury Bells, which, when they were first cultivated were called Coventry Bells, because according to the herbalist Henry Lyte they grew wild in the fields around Coventry. Parkinson said they did *not* grow wild there but only in gardens. At that time Canterbury Bells were *C. trachelium,* the native Nettle-leaved Bellflower and were given the name because the bell flowers resembled those carried by the pilgrims who visited Canterbury. Gerard, too, called Canterbury Bells by the Coventry label.

Like the Dianthus and the Primula families the Campanulas are a large group of a few good garden flowers which may be from other countries, and then an enormous quantity of species, a few of which are cultivated, mainly in the rock garden. As is often the case a lot of the rock garden species are quite difficult and are appreciated by collectors only. I'm afraid difficulty can rate as a virtue to the really enthusiastic Alpine gardener. On the whole, though, Campanulas are among the easiest plants to manage and apart from the few rockery 'miffs' will flower almost anywhere with the greatest freedom. They are not particular as to soil though naturally a warm, well-drained loam suits them better than cold clay.

It is a pity we have not more species for the border. *C. persicifolia* is a delightful summer plant and as with nearly all the family you can have blue flowers or white. Height is variable, but generally up to two feet, though I have seen a catalogue that claims three feet. At 1½ to 2 feet, groups should not need staking and that is an advantage. They get a bit untidy in late summer but if you have the patience to nip off the dead flowers, which is a sticky business, they will give a fresh crop almost as good as the first.

If you would like a really tall specimen you should grow *C. pyramidalis*. This used to be grown for greenhouse decoration and was a favourite in cottage windows where the stems were tied down as they grew to arched canes in graceful curves. Sounds as if it could look odd but well-grown specimens can be very impressive and they are sure winners in the pot-plant section of the village Flower Show.

C. pyramidalis is listed as hardy, but I have an idea it is not as hardy as it might be and in cold and northern gardens it will die out in hard winters. It grows to five feet or taller in rich soil and a good group makes an impressive sight at the back of a border. It is almost certain to need staking in the average garden.

C. glomorata is a wild native and in some parts of the country is so common that I cannot see it will do any harm if you dig up the odd plant and transfer it to your garden. If you have a conscience about doing that you can always collect seeds, since nearly all the bell flowers are easy to grow from seed. Of course the nursery will sell you *C. glomorata* but it is fun to have a few flowers in the garden you have hunted down for yourselves. The nursery plants will probably have larger flowers than the wild ones but if you feed the latter and coddle them up a bit there will not be much difference in the final results. The flowers are borne in clusters on the top of one foot stems. If you are looking for them I think the best hunting ground is the south-east and you are likely to be more successful south of the Thames than north of it. That gives a clue to its culture; indeed, I have known it, in cold gardens, to grow like a weed under a south-west wall, while plants moved to an open border soon disappeared.

C. lactiflora is tall, anything over three feet, with pale blue flowers. As a rule older plants die out but generally they seed themselves freely.

C. carpatica, which has nothing to do with carpeting but comes from the Carpathians, is a lovely little plant about a foot high that looks well and does well when grown in a large group at the front of the border.

There are a few more border types but they are not often found in lists and are either not remarkably good plants or are similar to the ones I have mentioned or not as good.

A closely related plant which I believe was at one time included in the Campanulaceae but has now been given a generic name of its own is *Platycodon grandiflorum*. The common name is Balloon Flower because the unopened buds do bulge out rather like balloons. These are easy to raise from seed and since they grow about a foot high you need a good group to make a show, so from seeds they should be grown rather than from plants at three or four shillings each. When the flowers are open they are the usual bellflower shape, but wide and flat rather than deep. There is a variety with pink flowers but I have not grown it.

The Campanula you see trailing from pots in cottage windows is *C. isophylla*. It is one of the easiest to grow and much loved, but alas it is not hardy!

Among the Alpine species are many gay and pretty flowers that can be useful, even valuable, in many parts of the garden. Most of them trail, all of the easier ones spread and you can have them on dry walls, as edgings to paths, in sinks, window boxes or vases, or as dot plants in paved gardens. If you are careful not to buy some treasure that will yield only two priceless bells in a season, the whole tribe will flower with astonishing generosity, covering large areas with such a wealth of blue that the flowers are touching each other so closely you can hardly see the leaves.

To get a good idea of what choice there is you really ought to visit an Alpine nursery when the plants are in flower, which is usually early summer. I have been looking through a catalogue list to help me pick a few of the best and there are about fifty! A lot of these are named garden varieties, but even then . . .

So here are a few I grow myself.

C. portenschlagiana, which is sometimes sold under the much easier name of *C. muralis* is excellent. It is practically evergreen and has, literally, thousands of sky-blue flowers on a good-sized patch. I have found it does well anywhere and it is a fair weed-smotherer, though not completely successful in that occupation.

C. poshcharskyana is another good spreader. It is worth learning the name so as to be able to ask for it.

I think the nurserymen get the names a bit mixed sometimes (who can blame them!) because I have had plants called *C. pulla,* *C. pulloides* and *C. pusilla* all bearing very similar flowers. However any of them are delightful and have tiny bells hung on three-inch stems. This is the type for a small space in the paved garden, and of course they are even better when they are grown at eye-level, say on a wall.

C. arvatica I only mention here as one of the *not* easy ones and nine out of ten planted would surely die after the first season. But some people *like* a struggle.

Among useful Alpine types are *C. garganica, C. turbinata,* and *C. rotarvatica* which is a hybrid.

For those who enjoy gardening in windows or in the greenhouse I would say some of the less easy Campanulas are well worth trying. Many of them are not really too difficult, but they do find our winters, changing from wet to cold and then to damp warmth a bit trying.

They are not alone in that!

Chapter 16: A FEW OF THE OTHERS

I am now in the position of a man who has invited to his party everyone who cares to come and then finds he has not room for all who want to come. This book could go on and on . . . and on! I started merrily with the flowers I felt could not be left out of anybody's garden; the essential ones, so to speak, but I grow others besides the ones I have mentioned and I have a great many which are in some ways more important garden plants. For instance I rate the Christmas Rose which I have not mentioned (yet) higher than the simple old Sunflower, which I have.

And then there are readers with favourites of their own which I have not included. I could be drummed out of the gardening fraternity by ignoring Scabious or Anchusa or any of the Viola tribe.

So here I will deal briefly with a few favourites that have been passed over so far and may I be forgiven for omitting all the others I really shall not have room for.

The Anchusa is a lovely plant with blue flowers like a Forget-me-not, only very much larger. There is no difficulty in growing it. I find it does better in warm light soil than in heavy stuff, though probably all plants do except the bog lovers. *A. semper-virens* was grown by Gerard and lives up to its name; it is on record that it was planted in the Tradescants' garden in 1656 and was still doing well in 1749. They used to make a red dye from the roots of *A. tinctoria* and it was used as a rouge. 'The Gentle-women of France do paint their faces with these roots' (Gerard). The dye had other uses, one of which was to give a good colour to Port wine—and even to wine that was *not* Port!

In my own garden I have an old-fashioned variety that was

found in a cottage garden somewhere, but the most showy and the one most recommended for general planting is the one called Dropmore, generally known by the full name of Anchusa, Dropmore variety.

Aquilegia is the Columbine, a native plant that has been mentioned in literature since the earliest times. A curious fact is that there is a very early reference to it in a recipe: 'Gelly coloured with columbine flowers.' Well, the plant belongs to the Ranunculacaeae and nearly every member of the family is risky if eaten and some I would regard as deadly. So jelly with Columbine flowers in it is the sort of thing you might have expected on the menu of a Borgia banquet—if you had been unpopular with them. Columbine certainly figured in medicines, as many poisonous plants have been, but Linnaeus gave a warning that children had lost their lives through taking an overdose. It is a very easy plant to grow, and does grow everywhere, self-sown seedlings springing up all over the garden. The long-spurred hybrids are the most common in cultivation, but this is a plant that hybridises so freely that you can start with a fine group of the new hybrids and in a few years find the garden full of the wild short-spurred type.

Aquila is eagle; columba is dove. A curious contrast in names.

As I am keeping this chapter to some sort of alphabetical order Bergenia had better come next though some gardeners and a few lists still call it *Saxifraga cordifolia*. Elephant's Ear is the common name, which it got because of the large glossy leaves. It is not widely used but is a good-tempered, easy thing, especially for a damp or shady spot. In favourable climates it will flower very early in the year; in fact I think my father classed it as a winter-flowering plant. The flowers are a good strong pink and are borne in large, loose heads. The best-known variety is Apple Blossom, though the colour is richer than you will see on most Apple trees.

The Foxglove is Digitalis and the drug so useful in certain heart conditions is made from the leaves. On the whole, although it is a handsome plant, it is perhaps better left to the hillsides and hedgerows. I don't know if it is a habit peculiar to my part of the country but it covers the hills when the trees are cut down. You will have a wood full of Bluebells; the trees are cut and the next thing you know is that there are far fewer Bluebells but the whole area is a mass of Foxgloves. So it looks as if they are not plants for shade and seeds must remain fertile and waiting for the sun for years.

Some good garden hybrids in white and yellow have been raised and these are worth planting. But the plants are true biennials and seed themselves freely. Many of these will revert to the original purple. But they are handsome and in garden soil very vigorous, so as long as they are not endangering other plants I leave them alone, and I get about as many whites as reds. You would think such tall spikes would need support but I have never staked a Foxglove. Perhaps that is because the bells hang down so do not hold the rain. The plant was once used in ointment for sores but generally the herbalists gave it little attention. It was used, though, because it was through knowing of its use in dropsy by a Shropshire 'wise woman' that Dr William Wittering was able to isolate the drug.

Eryngium maritimum is the botanical name of our native Sea Holly and it is such a handsome plant with its thistle-like, metallic blue flowers that many people like a few in the garden. It is definitely a plant for light soils; in fact by the seaside it is often found near or even on sand dunes, so if you have a really barren thirsty corner this is the plant to try. The roots are scented and in the old days were held to have all sorts of useful virtues. There is a long list in most of the herbals and the one in Gerard is typical. They 'are exceeding good to be given to old and aged people that are consumed and withered with age, and which want natural moisture.' They were used also in aphrodisiacs which is why Falstaff associated 'eringoes' with 'kissing comfits'.

Galega is Goats' Rue because it was believed that if used in their feed it increased their production of milk. It is a handsome plant with light green pea-style leaves and small purple pea-shaped flowers. A pretty thing but it took up so much room in my border that I banished it to a piece of wild garden where it can grow as tall and spread as wide as it likes. It is related to *G. tinctoria* from which the dye indigo is made, and another species has an intoxicating ingredient. By bruising the plant and throwing it into water fish are said to be drugged and come floating to the surface, but

I cannot trace if this is true, nor where it is done. There is a white-flowered variety which is quite pretty.

Two of the varieties of Geum are almost essential border plants. They are Mrs Bradshaw, which is bright red and the yellow Lady Stratheden. There are others but these two are both pretty and reliable. They do best in a warm rich loam that is not too heavy and they have the virtues of a long flowering season and not needing staking. They should be planted in good numbers to give the best effect. They have not been English border plants for long, having been introduced from South America in the first half of the last century. Our own wild flower, Herb Benet is related, and this, I am told, has aromatic roots which, long ago, were dried and placed among clothes to keep moths away. They were also used to flavour spirits, especially gin. Herb Benet was originally *Herba benedicta*, the Blessed Herb because 'where the root is in the house, the devil can do nothing, and flies from it.'

Well, we don't need Herb Benet because as the roadman said to me recently, 'All them clever chaps have said there ain't no devil no more.' Did he say it a shade regretfully? Like a lot of the old country people he liked the black separated from the white, then you knew where you were.

As for

> 'Long-legged beasties
> And things that go bump in the night'

anybody living near popular air routes may well say 'Good Lord, deliver us.'

Herb Benet is one of my least troublesome weeds. Perhaps I'll stick to it.

The Hollyhock is in Latin *Althea* but the former title is the more familiar. This has been grown in gardens for many hundreds of years and is mentioned in the fifteenth century manuscript poem *Feate of Gardening* by Ion Gardiner whose name sounds as if it could be a pen-name. Hollyhock has been grown for so long that nobody knows where it came from. It grows freely in Palestine so there is a theory that the Crusaders may have brought back some seeds. Most of the well-known herbalists and gardeners grew it and have left their descriptions of it, but though John

Evelyn records that the leaves were used as pot-herbs it does not seem to have become a popular vegetable. I cannot find any reference to it as a medicinal plant, but an attempt was made early in the nineteenth century to use the fibres to weave into a fabric. Nothing came of that but it was found that a blue dye could be made from the plant.

At one time the Hollyhock looked like becoming a Florists' Flower, with all the strict rules as to size, shape, markings and so on that those unfortunates suffered from. But a worse fate over-took it. About 1870 the Hollyhock rust appeared and it became so difficult to grow healthy plants that they lost their popularity. It is impossible to know, without getting the seedsmen to make out a popularity poll, how widely the flower is grown at present. I think it is not one of the first favourites, but it is a very lovely flower when grown in large gardens or against walls. I grew it for some years until the rust caught up with me and the plants became so miserable-looking that our parting seemed inevitable. However more by accident than good management I found, not a cure for the rust (though flowers of sulphur does not do it any good) but at least a way of giving the plant a good chance to cope with the enemy. It was simple really: very heavy dressings of farmyard manure. The plants thrived on that and became so vigorous that the little rust that did appear caused very little harm indeed.

I think I found out something then and that was that very well-fed, healthy plants are much less susceptible to diseases than the ill-fed ones which are what this manure-less age is giving us.

Commonsense, really! In general I suppose the rule holds good for us too.

The Oriental Poppy, *Papaver orientale*, is a lovely border plant with huge blooms in a variety of shades of pink and red as well as white. It is one of the easiest of plants and though the flowers are not long-lived they come over quite a long period. If the stems are dipped in boiling water they are good cut flowers.

Shirley Poppies are among the most brilliant annuals we have and they were developed about 1880 by the Rev. W. Wilks, who must have been a very modest man, calling them after his parish rather than after himself.

In my garden Iceland Poppies grow in such profusion that they are practically weeds. Yet they are so bright and so gay in early summer and give such large patches of brilliant yellow that I leave them a few rough patches—they thrive on paths, even in a crack on a wall—and let them flower as they will. And where they *are* invaders we dig out the tough, thong-like roots.

Papaver somniferum is the Opium Poppy. All the family is suspect to some degree but this is the real Black Sheep. There are all sorts of legends about it, a typical one being that it was created by Somnus, the god of sleep, to alleviate the woes of Ceres and allow her to slumber.

That is the clue to the whole story. Since man can remember, a pain-relieving, sleep-giving drug, opium, has been made from the sap. In fairness let it be said that not all who, over the centuries, have made the drug, recognised the danger. In this country for instance in the early nineteenth century the plant was a commercial crop and something like 50,000 pounds of opium were made and used annually. The medicine made from it was laudanum and it could be bought freely at the apothecary's shop. It was natural that people in pain, not recognising the risk, used it for anything from toothache to a bout of insomnia.

You cannot help wondering. It was given to fretful children: did they all become addicts? There is even a mention that 'it was used instead of tea by the poorer class of female in Manchester and other manufacturing towns.'

Was this some very weak form. Or does this partly explain the lower expectation of life a century or two ago?

Then there are the well-known classic cases: de Quincy, Coleridge, Edgar Allan Poe, Elizabeth Barrett Browning and other writers who had great flashes of brilliance followed by the dark shadows of despair and obscurity.

In the hands of doctors opium has yielded some of the most valuable drugs known to medicines. In the wrong hands the same drugs are as safe as dynamite handled by drunks.

The sad part of the story is that, in spite of the completely destructive powers of misuse, there are people who, purely for gain, will manufacture and distribute—well, apparently anything.

H bombs or heroin (a derivative of opium). Only pay us enough for it and you can have it!

To something more pleasant. *Polygonatum multiflorum* is Solomon's Seal. The name is generally believed to be due to the Hebrew characters you can see on the roots if you cut through them, but Gerard said it was on account of the wonderful healing (sealing) properties of the root which you first smash up and then use either as a poultice or drink in ale, when it 'soddereth and glewith togither the bones in a very short space and very strangely.' It was good for bruises and from a distilled lotion of the juices you obtained a face-wash to clear the complexion. If there had been a family quarrel women could use it to get rid of black eyes quickly. Years ago women, often with plenty of poorly-paid maids to help them, had time to make these simple remedies (hence 'simples') in their still rooms (distilling rooms). But today 'the world is too much with us' and we rush around going and getting nowhere very fast. And so these wonderful remedies go untried. What a pity! Mind I expect nine out of ten of them are a heap of old rubbish, but the tenth—ah, the tenth would give us unequal complexions, restore our hair, make us as strong as lions and renew our youth! Or wouldn't it?

I do remember very clearly when I was a little boy having a festering sore on my hand. The festering and the pain went but the sore grew and grew. An old man noticed it and he said, Get me this and that—a few very simple ingredients—and I'll make you something to clear that. I did and it did. But he would not tell me what he made.

As a plant I used to rather undervalue Solomon's Seal. Then I suddenly *saw* it and I have liked it ever since. The stems arch widely and are as graceful as any plant could possibly be. Put two apexes together and you will not see a finer arch in any building. The little green-tipped white flowers hang from every leaf axil like fairy bells, the leaves are strong and handsome. It is a lovely plant in the garden and it is lovely in a vase and when the flowers have gone you can still use them to show off some other flower.

The plant should be grown in a colony where it will increase. It likes damp soil rich in humus. It is excellent for the bog garden and if you can give it plenty of moisture it will do well in light shade, even under trees.

Red Hot Pokers should have come under K being Kniphofias, but much as I agree that Herr Kniphof is worthy of honour because he published a herbal of twelve folio volumes in 1746 I find the earlier name Tritoma trips more easily off the tongue, and if we say Red Hot Pokers everybody knows what we mean.

The plants came from Africa, from the Cape first, about 1700. There are yellow species and there are orange-red ones; there are tall ones and dwarf ones; there are some that flower in June and there are some for September. I prefer the latter because they make such a fiery blaze just as so many other plants are beginning to look a little bit tired. They have been liked by some gardeners, regarded with suspicion by others who felt that such gaudiness might be 'violation of good taste'.

If I may parody the well-known lines

> 'Tobacco is a filthy weed: I like it'

then I say

> 'Tritoma is a gaudy weed: I like it.'

The strange thing is that every authority I know says they are slightly tender—they were actually treated as greenhouse plants at Kew when they were first introduced—and are safer if covered with some loose material in winter; in my heavy clay and our hard winters they thrive without the least protection. But there you are, some plants like some people, have peculiar ways.

I do not think that in the chapter on Daisy flowers I mentioned the Scabious. Of course, as this book is still in manuscript it would be the easiest thing in the world to go back and include it tidily—but I love to write as I talk (and garden!) wandering about from one thing to another. So it shall come here.

There is not a lot to say except that it seems to want a light soil. I have lost many a good plant in a hard winter. It is lovely in a large group towards the front of the border and it is splendid for cutting. The first plants in northern Europe were very dark in colour. The light blue ones such as Clive Greaves are varieties of

S. caucasia, which was found in the Caucasian Mountains about 1800.

The native flower is almost as fine as the cultivated ones. This used to have the name of Devils Bit Scabious and I remember my father telling me when I was a small boy that the devil bit the root, presumably to destroy it, but it was so bitter he spat it out. How these old stories last! That one was in the *Grete Herbal* in 1526 and the reason the devil bit the plant was because he was jealous of its many virtues.

The wild Scabious grew, and still does, to perfection in the Pembrokeshire hedges. On my cold hillside it is never seen (though there is a tiny species among the rocks in the hills). And there you have a very rough guide as to what you may grow with ease in your gardens. If the wild species are among your common wild flowers then you are likely to find it easy. If you never see it anywhere you may have a tussle to get it to flourish in the garden.

I have had many species under many names, probably inaccurate, of Sedums in the rock garden for about as long as I have been gardening, but for the border you may, if you like it, grow Orpine, *S. telphium* which you can collect in many places, ranging from the Berkshire Downs to the seaside. Then you can dig it up on Midsummer Day and hang it from your kitchen ceiling (from a beam if you have one) and it will stay green until Christmas. 'Those that hang it up . . . they shall be troubled with no Distemper so long as it remains green.'

The Sedum I grow at the front of the border is the Japanese *S. spectabile,* a much larger plant than any of the wild species, with light green, fleshy leaves and large heads of flowers in autumn. On a sunny day the flowers are covered with insects; butterflies love it so much that their wings may give it more colour than its own lavender flowers.

Most of the Sedums seem harmless for they have been used in salads and as medicines. They were used for gout in Anglo-Saxon times. Our native yellow Stonecrop, *S. acre,* once had the country name of Welcome-home-husband-though-never-so-drunk, and I really would like to know who gave it that name and *why.*

Spiraeas may be shrubs, such as the purple Antony Waterer,

and very good, very easy shrubs they are; but for the most part the herbaceous species are plants for the bog garden. The best-known is, I am sure, our native Meadowsweet, S. *ulmaria,* and though the hawthorn-type scent can be very heady it is delightful in small quantities. It is seldom a plant of gardens but self-sown seedlings have appeared in mine and where it is not in the way I have left it alone and it does not look out of place.

In an old Pembrokeshire garden I found a plant with most attractive fern-like leaves growing in rosettes. It was winter, the rosettes were small and I thought it would be useful for the background of my rock garden. It turned out to be a Spiraea (or first cousin) *Filipendula hexapetala,* and it was *not* a plant for *any* part of the rock garden. The rosettes of leaves are huge in summer, overgrowing everything in reach and the heads of pink-white feathery flowers are on stems at least two feet tall. But at the back of the border or in the bog garden it is a beauty. It has two great virtues; the leaves stay handsome nearly all the year round, and nobody knows what it is (being a rather old-fashioned cottage flower) so everybody wants a root, which is flattering to my good taste if nothing else.

The tall Spiraea is a handsome plant for a large border, otherwise it is better grown where it can form a group. Since the bare stems stay erect, brown and handsome through winter it might be as well to use it where one would use a shrub or a group of them, though of course it is not at all shrub-like, being truly herbaceous. It is very easy to grow, either near water or away from it.

The only point to be wary of is that in buying it you do not get something you do not want because the botanists have rung the changes in names and what your grandfather called one thing you may well know as something else, and the nurseryman may not use either label. Spiraea belongs to the Rose family, while Astilbe is one of the Saxifrage tribe. The business is complicated because there are short and tall members in both species. I think though if you ask for Astilbes you will get the shorter bushy plants with flowers varying from white to pink, and these are ideal for the side of the pool.

The one you see with tall pyramidal plumes of flowers about

six feet tall is a relation of the Spiraeas called Rodgersia, and the full name of the commonest is *R. aesculifolia*. The other tall 'Spiraea' is *S. aruncus* and the flowers of this are flattish not spires.

My alphabetical list is getting a bit out of hand but Lysimachia is not a familiar name to most gardeners, though I could call it Twopenny Grass, or Moneywort . . . or one or two more names. Do not confuse those with Lunaria or Penny Flowers, though that is a biennial well worth growing. Lysimachia is not an aristocrat but it deserves a place in any garden. It is pretty; it will grow, literally, almost anywhere, even under trees unless the shade is very dense; and it is invaluable to make a good show in the border or to brighten that dull corner where nothing else will grow. The stems crowd close together and one plant will soon spread to a fine clump. They grow about two feet high and are clothed all the way up with rich yellow flowers, open-bell in shape, about the size of a shilling. It does so well so easily that many who do grow it forget that even the humblest of plants are a lot better if they get a bit of food—so give it at least a generous handful of fertiliser.

Its close relation with exactly the same flowers in sixpenny size, and exactly the same nicknames, is the more familiar Creeping Jenny. This is *L. nummularia*, while our tall one is *L. vulgaris*, Yellow Loosestrife. It is not related to Purple Loosestrife.

L. vulgaris has been grown in gardens since the sixteenth century, perhaps earlier, when they used the smoke of the dried plant to drive away serpents and kill flies.

It is, apart from driving away serpents, a very pleasant plant that deserves to be better known.

'When Jupiter had turned the young damosell Io, whom he tenderly loved, into a Cow, the earth brought forth this floure for her food; which being made for her sake, received the name from her: and thereupon it is thought the Latines called it Viola.'

That is one of the earliest legends about all our Violas, Pansies and Violets, and though there are others that one is the prettiest so we will not confuse matters.

There are species in many countries but our own little native which the first Elizabethans knew and liked so well is about as attractive as any. It is from those times that the plant seems to have gained in popularity; constant crossing and selection have led to the striking forms of Violas and Pansies you can raise today from a few pennyworth of seeds. There is little or no botanical difference in the various species; the gardener as a rule calls the self-coloured flowers Violas, while the marked ones which often resemble faces—whence the Tudor name of Three-faces-in-a-hood—are Pansies, the 'pansies, that's for thoughts' of poor mad Ophelia.

The plant has had two histories: one as a medicine, the other as a garden flower.

As a medicine it was 'good for all inflamations, especially of the sides and lungs; they (the flowers) take away the hoarseness of the chest, the ruggednesse of the winde-pipe and jawes and take away thirst.'

And of course from wild Pansies (Hearts Ease) was made a notable heart medicine.

There were other medicinal uses and given a little faith no doubt they did a little good.

As a flower, constant hybridising went on and it is interesting to note that a breeder who did great things for Viola was a manager of Dicksons whose name was James Grieve. One of our best-known early dessert apples bears his name.

He was working on the plants soon after 1860, but this was quite late in their history for the flowers had already become Florists' Flowers with their Shows, their rules and their Societies, early in the century.

The inevitable happened. There was a tremendous wave of enthusiasm for the perfect blooms, the Black Country, of all places, being the centre of the cult; the wave receded, the Shows died out, and we were left with some very pleasant flowers which many gardeners did not bother to grow.

For the gardens of the present here are flowers that are easy to grow from seed and are not at all demanding. You can grow Pansies of a great size, or if size does not appeal, much more modest flowers, by avoiding the giant strains. They are seldom imposing enough for borders but large drifts elsewhere can be lovely, though to keep the display going right through summer all dead flowers must be removed. The plants are not long-lived as a rule but they seed themselves freely. They are good for window-boxes or any other containers and a few plants in pots will generally give a good account of themselves in a cool or cold greenhouse. As edgings to beds or paths they are excellent, but for any beds containing strong colours, such as Roses, it is better to grow the single colours (Violas) in white or some very quiet shade. I have seen Roses underplanted with white Violas and it was a very pleasing combination, apart from the fact that the Violas did their share in weed-smothering.

Very few gardeners cultivate Violets in any quantities nowadays but besides the lovely colours of the best varieties the scent is so fine that it is a pity they are neglected. They are easy to grow in a light peaty soil and very old manure and if you have a spare frame they can be flowered in winter. They were, it is claimed, the favourite flowers of Queen Alexandra and from her the best-known variety, Princess of Wales, took its name.

I would not go so far as to say I have saved the best until last, but it is by no means the least, either.

There are a number of Hellebores, mostly whitish of petal but some so tinted that they appear almost green, while others are a purple shade. The best is the white *Helleborus niger,* the Christmas Rose.

This is not an easy plant to establish in the garden. Many are sold on the plant stalls of the multiple stores, generally in not very robust health and often at the wrong time of the year. The enthusiastic gardener with visions of those dazzling white flowers buys one, or a dozen, takes them home and plants them. Then they die. To be quite fair my one fine plant is a survivor of a bundle I bought at a stall for sixpence each.

Buy plants from a reliable nurseryman who sells his plants in containers and make sure the plants are established, not freshly-divided stock. Prepare sites by digging in a lot of old manure, compost, peat and leaf-mould. The sites should enjoy full light all winter and shade or semi-shade all summer. This is not as hard as it sounds because you can grow them along the back of a border behind a lot of taller plants that will keep all the sun off them, for all the world like a row of tall boys with some small ones sheltering behind. Then in autumn you move the dead stems of the tall stuff to the compost heap and there are your Christmas Roses out in the daylight again and enjoying such sunlight as we are likely to have from November to March.

How long you will wait for flowers after planting is anybody's guess. You may have some the first year; you may have to wait four or five. Early in winter put some slug bait among the plants, then cover them with sheets of glass; I put mine tent-wise, not because the flowers are not perfectly hardy, but to prevent their being splashed by soil.

The flowers will start any time. Some years there will be a few at the time you move the dead stuff in front; other years it may be long after Christmas. I am sorry: I cannot state anything firmly, Christmas Roses are like that.

But when the blooms appear you will reap your reward for it seems unbelievable that flowers of such exquisite purity and dazzling whiteness should appear at any time, let alone in the cold hardness of winter.

If you would like them in vases, and you will because the weather will be so wretched that you certainly will not want to stand in the garden admiring them, then pull them with as much stalk as you can, make several slits up the base of each stem and get them into water as soon as you can. In a few days the pretty stamens will drop, but apart from that the blooms will last in water for weeks or even months. They will last longer in cool rooms than in warm ones, but as usual they are quite unpredictable and are likely to do exactly what you do not expect them to do.

Good colonies of *Helleborus niger* are comparatively rare in gardens. And that is a great pity because there is not one gardener in a hundred whose winters would not be brightened by them.

The plant, as a garden plant, is very, very old. The best-known legend is that an angel made them spring out of the earth for a girl who had no gift to offer at the Nativity.

It was noted for its magical properties, was a protection against evil spirits, and from the time of the shepherd Melampus, who used it to cure the daughters of Praetus, King of Argus, was a famous medicine to cure madness. It grew widely at Anticyra near Corinth and the Greeks had a saying 'Go to Anticyra' which was a hint to their friends that they were not right in the head. Some tribes used it for tipping arrows because they thought it made the meat of the animals they killed more tender. It is poisonous, yet it was used to break spells and enchantments; bewitched animals could be restored to health by inserting a bit of root in their ears. The faith in its efficiency against bewitchment lasted in our country until at least the nineteenth century, and cottagers grew it by their doors so that nothing evil could enter. Gerard said that a medicine made from it 'is good for mad and furious men, for melancholy, dull and heavie persons, and briefly, for all those that are troubled with black choler and molested with melancholy.'

There were cures in plants for everything in those times of faith. Oh, happy days!

And so the garden goes on. No sooner is one thing over than we are looking for its successor. Always something to anticipate happily, always something to expect, always something to enjoy.

Solomon knew all about it three thousand years ago. None of us could say it better:

Arise, O north wind; and come thou south; blow upon my garden, that the spices thereof may flow out.

INDEX